'a society that has lost its soul'
(Michael Henderson, writing of England
in *The Daily Telegraph*, August 2001)

'Football had a soul where it now keeps its wallet.... Teams outside of the magic circle that is the Premier League must contemplate a different existence....'
(Michael Parkinson, *The Daily Telegraph*, April 2002)

'Money has destroyed a proper league. The Premiership has become a competition that mocks the tens of thousands of loyal, traditional lovers of the game.'
(David Miller, *The Daily Telegraph*, January 2003)

BY THE SAME AUTHOR

Jaunt Account
Games Beyond Frontiers
Pitch Black

RICHARD BRENTNALL

A DIFFERENT CORNER

Exploring Spanish Football

Matador
5 Weir Road
Kibworth Beauchamp
Leicester LE8 0LQ, UK
Tel: (+44) 116 279 2299
Fax: 0116 279 2277
Email: books@troubador.co.uk
Web: www.troubador.co.uk/matador

ISBN 978 1848761 452

British Library Cataloguing in Publication Data.
A catalogue record for this book is available from the British Library.

Typeset in 12pt Bembo by Troubador Publishing Ltd, Leicester, UK
Printed and bound in Great Britain by TJ International Ltd, Padstow, Cornwall

Matador is an imprint of Troubador Publishing Ltd

CONTENTS

Prologue

England and football are two things profoundly dear to my heart. In the past this was irrevocably so, but in recent years I've developed a love-hate relationship with both. I love England, but hate the way it's gone. I love football, but hate the way that's gone too.

So I contemplated a different existence, Michael; and went ahead, emigrating to Spain in late March 2007.

It was a decision both easy and difficult. It was easy because I had only myself to answer to and, at my stage of life, I really wanted a new lease of that. My disenchantment with my homeland facilitated the decision all the more. If I said it was difficult because I was forsaking the land of my bloodline, I'd be lying; hearts and souls are transportable and remain intact. It was difficult only because I'd no longer be able to see my beloved team every week nor my good and true, like-minded friends – but I'm keeping my season ticket, shall fly back once a month or so to use it, so that difficulty doesn't feel quite so sore.

So here I am, in a different corner of Europe.

Why am I disenchanted with England?

Where politics are concerned I'm a mere layman. But this layman would recognise the fundamental ideal of good health, to be able to learn, to be able to get around, and not to be abused. He most definitely recognises that the health service, the education system, the transport system and crime prevention in England are, in turn, sorely lacking, ridiculous, pathetic and (though not to criminals) frightening. As far as I can see, the only tangible achievement of President Blair's ten-year ego trip (that took him to Ulster where gangsters still rule, to the oil-rich Middle East where there's still mayhem, and to Washington to rub shoulders with a nincompoop) is no-smoking signs. Oh, but I do him a disservice. He's made England into a wonderfully harmonious multicultural society too....

It all goes beyond that, though. I became wholly dismayed by crassly uncivilised behaviour, rampant bad manners and (surely an emblem of lack of moral fibre) litter all over the place. By Jamaican youths posturing, hoods up even in eighty degrees, as black American gangstas innit, and white youths trying to be one of them. By what was thrust upon me upstairs on a filthy bus as 'music'. By nonentities' being thrust upon me as 'celebrities'. By political (and virtually anything ending in 'al') correctness. By a mollycoddling health-and-safety culture: 'Take Care On The Steps'. By boorish, aggressive youths spoiling my Friday nights. By boorish young females trying to convince the world that they're having a great partying time by screeching every word. By their awful tattoos. By self-centredness. By absence of conscience. By do-gooders trying to tell me that perpetrators are victims instead of punishing and deterring. England, in so many ways, has lost its identity, and I've moved away to ensure that I retain my own. Plus, I didn't want to end up being kicked to death by a crowd of young tossers should I have collared one for tossing a beer can into my front garden. Nor being stabbed for being a white man in Alum Rock in the hours of darkness. Nor, for that matter, being blown up in the name of Allah.

I fear that England, like its football, has now gone too far.

Why do I hate the way football's gone?

Once upon a time, football in England was raw and meaningful and played out upon a level playing field. In his 1964 autobiography *Determined To Win*, George Eastham rejoiced in the thought that 'we have at least thirty clubs virtually on a par'. Proof of that erstwhile level playing field is that, in the first fourteen seasons of my football-loving life, there were eleven different champions of England, and subsequently teams such as Nottingham Forest could come from nowhere to be champions of all Europe too. My club is West Bromwich Albion, which I love dearly and always shall. We've won only three trophies in my lifetime, but my salient point is this: the chance to embrace glory always used to be there for everyone, but today it's not, and it'll never present itself again to the likes of us. Football's new elitism and, thereby, its exclusivity, all based upon money, is now irreversible. I feel as though a door has been slammed in my face and padlocked from within. I feel the futility of it all. The magic has gone.

This isn't the England I grew up in, nor is it the football I fell in love with as a child.

○ ○ ○

Why Spain?

OK, as I pen these words, the sun is bathing the mountains, making Mijas village glisten and the distant Med twinkle, and it's also irresistibly cheering people's dispositions. There's a golf course less than five minutes' walk away too. But those – whilst wholly welcome and indeed quite crucial – are everyday factors in comparison with the deeper reasons. I didn't choose lightly my new lease of life.

Yes of course I wanted a good climate to aid my own disposition. But I wanted too a place in which to feel both at ease and enriched. As regards feeling at ease, Spain was hardly uncharted territory in that respect, and also I can clamber out of my bed here on a Saturday morning and still be at The Hawthorns for kick-off hour. I haven't come here, though, to lie on a beach, stagnate and see what's left of my life merely ebb away like a disinterested tide. The land I went to needed deeply to be fascinating and begging exploration: enriching.

Spain to me is indeed fascinating: geographically, historically and (even to a layman) politically. It's a different corner, for sure. Geographically it's as though it's divorced from the mainstream Continent, with a determined culture which emphasises that. Historically, whilst untouched by two world wars, this is from where explorers and *conquistadores* moulded South America. Politically, being less of a nation and more of a mini-continent where landscapes, climates, traditions and particular notions of nationalism are diverse, Spain has emerged from a very brutal civil war of merely seven decades ago, has clenched its teeth to embrace post-Francoism, but still simmers beneath the surface. Such divorce, exploration and simmering are fine by me.

And: football. I don't kid myself. The way football's gone of course hasn't sullied only England. Hearing any mention of Sepp Blatter or, especially, his awful Trinidadian ally Jack Warner will drive home that from the highest level. Since I've lived in southern Spain, all too many taxi drivers have told me that they don't like football as much as before, for two main reasons: it's all about money now, and all too many club presidents' personal gains are ill-gotten (including in the very murky area of construction). I've also, so far, come across only one taxi driver who supported the local club, Malaga; the others said that they were, rather inevitably, Barca or Real, though they'd never been to the Camp Nou or Bernabeu.

Nevertheless, I consider that the Spanish league is the best in Europe - and surely the world. My three main reasons are: the majority of the really top players are here; the tempo of the matches is no worse than in the English Premier League (and better than the riskless chess in Italy), while the technical and tactical expertise is visibly superior (players here can use both feet to control and keep the ball, and they think about optimum use); more clubs in Spain than in England haven't had that door slammed and padlocked.

So I've come to my different corner to experience, too,

another football scene. It might well become as dismaying and unenriching as English football. I can see one potential problem straightaway: the worst thing in football, to me, is cheating, and there's a culture in Spain of cutely engineering advantages (particularly penalty-kicks) through what I'd label as diving.

But what I know for certain is that I need, whether for better or worse, something different to feel inside where football's concerned. This will indeed be a journey of exploration.

So, if you reckon that the English Premiership is all-wonderful, this journey may not be for you. If you don't: climb aboard.

FIRST STEPS
Saturday 8ᵗʰ September

As the train from Fuengirola rattled on its way along the coast, I tried to remember the last time I'd seen a Spanish club side on its own soil in the flesh, and quickly realised that there hadn't been many such instances at all. In fact, for all that I'd watched numerous Spanish teams on their visits to England, today would be only my third time.

I could well remember my first, though, and not just because I'd never previously set foot in the country at all. For one thing, I'd managed to plummet through some rotting floorboards to end up half-naked in the thankfully deserted bar beneath, which, at four in the morning, had looked like a hundred-foot drop as I'd gurgled and clung to the last, useless chunk of decayed wood; another of us had fared much worse and ended up in hospital in Alicante with severe sunstroke. We'd all been of a certain age, in a good football age: August 1977.

It was an age when Albion's name still carried sufficient weight to see us invited to pre-season tournaments abroad. That one had pitted us against Dinamo Tbilisi of the Soviet Union who quite soon, with Chivadze and Kipiani to the fore, would demolish Liverpool in the European Cup; Beveren, who quite soon would twice be champions of Belgium; and the host club Hercules, who've still never lifted any meaningful Spanish trophy but ensured that they triumphed in that Trofeo Costa Blanca through blatant cheating. Not an auspicious introduction for myself where watching Spanish teams was concerned.

Whereas the season's leading marksman in Spain receives the *Pichichi* award that commemorates a legendary Athletic Bilbao goalscorer of the early twentieth century, the season's leading referee gets the *Guruceta* accolade, commemorating the country's supposedly finest ever who died in a car crash in 1987. Jose Emilio Guruceta Muro: someone who'd fuelled Barca fans' notion that the dice were loaded against them in favour of Real Madrid during the Franco years by awarding the visitors a highly dubious and crucial penalty-kick at the Camp Nou back in 1970 that provoked a riot (he was chased off the pitch) and infamy (the whole episode remains significant not only in Spanish football history but also for Catalonia); and someone who was most definitely bribed by Anderlecht fourteen years later. Nottingham Forest had taken a 2-0 advantage to Brussels for the second leg of their UEFA Cup semi-final, which they lost 0-3, but Paul Hart had a perfectly legitimate goal disallowed, Brian Clough labelled a penalty-kick awarded against Kenny Swain 'a travesty', and Forest were denied two spot-kicks of their own. Hans van Breukelen, Forest's goalkeeper, had thought there'd been 'something fishy going on'. There certainly was: in 1997 Anderlecht's president Roger van den Stock finally admitted that his father and predecessor, Constant, had paid the referee, Guruceta, the equivalent of £18,000.

The final of the Trofeo Costa Blanca had meant nothing in comparison, but it was fixed all right. Guruceta gave Hercules two ridiculous penalty-kicks, waved unwarranted yellow cards at our lot, actually reduced us to nine men, and even flashed a red at Ronnie Allen too when all our manager was guilty of was approaching the touchline to substitute Willie Johnston, who'd become even friskier than usual. This wasn't fishiness, it was barely believable blatancy. After the fiasco (and a 5-1 scoreline) we saw Guruceta at a pavement table drinking and chuckling into the night with two rather fetching young women. Ironically, sat with us nearby was a group of Albion players that included a young Bryan ("we shoulda broken a few bloody legs") Robson, and Johnston, who flashed a few handsigns at the cheat when he glanced our way. After Guruceta and his two escorts departed, Albion's physio George Wright, having looked at the right knee I'd twisted in my plummet, left for bed too, so enabling the rest of us to repair to the players' hotel, the Gran Sol, and drink till dawn in its conference room, the concierge suitably in on the act. Yes, that was an age when top players and fans could still make a social connection. No-one around that table, not even Len Cantello, was wearing a £32,000 necklace.

My second time, fifteen months later, was a much more wholesome experience; indeed, it was the proudest I've ever felt as an Albion supporter. The result was only a 1-1 draw but, after we'd equalised an early goal in that UEFA Cup first-leg match, we'd totally dominated Kempes, Bonhof and the whole lot of them in the second half with a brand of football that was both powerful and sumptuous, consigning Valencia to submission in their own backyard – so much so that the entire full house stood to a man at the final whistle to salute us, the ovation prolonged, reverberating and tingling. We really should have won the UEFA Cup that season, and the English championship too, but didn't, and Laurie Cunningham's bewitching performance that night in Valencia alerted Real Madrid, for whom he left us in the summer. It was the beginning of the end for Albion as a force to be reckoned with.

○ ○ ○

I noticed three Malaga shirts join the train at Benalmadena but saw no others when I alighted. Two days earlier another taxi driver had expressed support for Malaga but he hadn't known on which day of the weekend they'd be playing. He'd said that many folk were interested only if they were in the top division. That was probably the case, too, for Jose, despite what he'd asserted to me on the evening I'd made his acquaintance back in May, albeit while everyone had been getting half-cut. A sturdy man in his thirties, clipped beard complementing black locks, a builder by trade and with fair English, he'd detested then how people from the area could lick the boots of big clubs instead of supporting their local team. He was, he emphasised, a *Malaguista* because this was his *pueblo* (home turf). But his brother David had dawdled into a Fuengirola bar and when I'd asked him if Jose was going to the Cordoba game on Saturday, David had chuckled and said: "No. He goes only when *La Primera!*" I'd also cast my mind back three months to recall the night that the championship had been decided when Real, Barca and (though rather tenuously by that stage) Sevilla had all been in contention on the last day. I'd watched the Real-Mallorca match on television and the Cuba Libre bar, like so many in Fuengirola that night, had been awash with people in Real Madrid colours, who afterwards lorded around the town. Had this been, say, somewhere in the Black Country, I'd thought to myself at the time, and awash with gloating Manchester United 'fans', others with homespun allegiances would surely have done something about that....

Those three Malaga shirts conveniently, since I hadn't a clue where the stadium was, led the way. Along the Avenida De La Rosaleda, skirting the Guadalmedina riverbed, surprisingly no bars to slake my thirst, over bridges, and after twenty-five minutes' stroll I was almost there. It had been an entirely straight road, in direct contrast to Malaga CF's convoluted lineage and indeed to its current predicament. And I wondered just how many, or how few, would bother to turn up to support them, for still those three shirts were the only ones I'd seen among the few folk making their way up that road, and the six-thirty kick-off was now just an hour away.

On the wide approach to the stadium, though, a vast car park on my right was filling up and then ahead I could see hundreds of people milling around. This was match day now all right, and an Andalucian derby too, such locale somehow underlined by palm trees greeting this *extranjero* as he made for the ticket windows through the throng past stalls selling beer, water, various nibbles and, wonderfully, cigars. This wasn't England: no paranoia nor social pariahs here. A couple of years earlier I'd visited my prospective new home to come across several bars in Fuengirola displaying no-smoking signs as the Spanish authorities had decided to so regulate, based upon square metreage. A couple of months afterwards I'd revisited and those same bars now allowed smoking. Frank, a Mancunian who runs a bar on the Paseo Maritimo, naturally appreciative of what deters custom, had told me: "There's some very imaginative tape measures around here." Basically the authorities had tried, given up, and turned a blind eye. Myself, I can appreciate a no-smoking enforcement in theatres, cinemas, libraries, whatever. But in football grounds? In the dissipating open air? Where particularly tense people need to assuage their anxiety? (People who have to stomach their unassuaged anxiety over ninety-plus minutes because they care, while others miss the action to fetch picnics and then leave with ten minutes to go to pollute all around with their petrol fumes.) But I was in Spain now; although I didn't buy any cigars because I had my cigarettes.

Twenty-odd Cordoba fans, bedecked in green and white, came hurtling through the throng in horn-blowing self-announcement, heading for the beer stalls. I was in Spain now; this self-announcement was wholly acceptable. When I turned to look, I saw back-patting, and no police.

I decided to treat myself, eased my way to the front of the squash, and forked out thirty-five euros for a place high in the Tribuna Stand. Now, this *extranjero* encountered a little difficulty. It wasn't so much the kids' wanting you to somehow get them inside too (I'd offered one a crisp only to have my naivety ridiculed), but the fact that gate nineteen was obstinately hiding, and there was no official around to ask other than the wrong turnstile operators who variously pointed me in opposite directions. But I finally arrived, via quite precipitous steps, in the correct area but not the right seat, on the back row overlooking the halfway line smack next to the Canal 2 Andalucia cameraman, lit a fag, and took stock. I also thumbed through a free club newspaper and a free match programme, quite a contrast to two and a half weeks earlier when I'd gone back to England to take in not only Albion's first home match of the season but also the Germany game at Wembley where a match programme there had creamed people for all of six quid.

I'm obviously a traditionalist. Yes of course you have to move with the times, with inevitable change, but I value tradition. I make a connection between tradition and soul. I think it'd been Otto Rehhagel, the German coach who fantastically led Greece to become champions of Europe in 2004 while Eriksson fannied around with supposedly superior players (multi-millionaires with only one useful foot), who'd said that all of these new stadia must have come from just one computerised blueprint: you could be here, there or anywhere now, whereas once upon a time you knew for sure where you were, Hamburg, Munich, wherever. Right on, Otto. Leaving out of the argument dear Lord Justice Taylor's recommendations, leaving out of the argument English football's chasing after a new well-monied consumer, and leaving out of the argument too that personally I can't equate watching my team with comfort in any case, since I'd much rather stand than squirm in my anxiety, must virtually all of those new English stadia be so utterly characterless? You could put black seats in the Walkers Stadium and be in Derby, you could put blue seats in Pride Park and be in Leicester, you could put red seats in either and be in Southampton. Just a dash of individualistic design, a point of traditional reference to the past, some *pueblo*-equivalent feature, would just about suffice: but no. Maybe that's the way preferred by the powers-that-be in England today: blob stadia populated by blob folk too shy to shout up and stand out, all overseen by satisfied Health And Safety, totally soulless.

So I lit another fag and gazed around. Was the Estadio La Rosaleda characterless or not so? Thirty years earlier I'd been inside perhaps my most characterful stadium of all: old Ibrox, with its grand Archibald Leitch main stand and two huge banks of end terracing, one roofless, the whole place timeless and oozing history and spiritual presence, evocative of a Morton dribble, a Baxter shimmy and all the countless legendary deeds forming the Rangers badge that bound the baying hordes of successive generations. For its character, old Ibrox was a ten. In its anonymity, Middlesbrough's Riverside was a zero.

La Rosaleda had had early problems. Building had begun in June 1936, but due to the Civil War (and Malaga had been committedly Republican) it wasn't completed until 1941. Upgraded for the 1982 World Cup, it'd finally arrived at its present form in the summer of 2006 with the completion of the Tribuna Stand in which I now sat. It was a two-tiered bowl of blue and white seating, but the ends were open to the elements (and, yes, it can rain violently on the Costa del Sol). High opposite to the right was perched the fourteenth-century Gibralfaro castle. To my left swept the sierra. I gave La Rosaleda a five.

I'd earlier given myself a headache trying to unravel that convoluted lineage. Unpicking a Moroccan rug would have been more straightforward.

Malaga Football Club had been formed in 1904 and changed its name, with the royal blessing of Alfonso XIII, to Real Malaga FC in 1927. In the meantime, in 1912, a rival club named FC Malagueno had started up. In 1930 Real Malaga FC became Malaga Sports Club. Three years later the rivals merged to form Club Deportivo Malacitano and eight years after that this new club began calling itself Club Deportivo Malaga. In 1948 it took over a junior club to act as its reserve team and renamed those reserves Club Atletico Malagueno. Eleven years on, and CA Malagueno separated from the parent club to register as an independent club in its own right.

CD Malaga's financial problems would become so acute that it ceased to exist come 1992. Once merely a reserve team, CA Malagueno now assumed the mantle of the city's football representation, and within a year had gained promotion to *Segunda Division B* (Spain's third level). But in 1994 CA Malagueno encountered severe problems both on the park (relegation back) and off it (almost, like CD Malaga before them, disappearing entirely). At this point the club, following a referendum among its members, changed its name to Malaga Club de Futbol, and two knights named Fernando Puche and Federico Beltron rode in to rescue it from bankruptcy. Such was its subsequent progress that in 1999 Malaga CF was promoted to the top division. Whereas the defunct CD Malaga had enjoyed twenty seasons in the *Primera Division*, this was of course new territory for the city's surviving club.

For six of their seven seasons in the top flight, without pulling up any trees, Malaga CF had acquitted themselves quite well despite, with financial difficulty forever lurking, being a selling club. In 2001 they finished as high as eighth, while in 2003, having knocked out Leeds United and AEK Athens along the way, they reached the quarter-finals of the UEFA Cup. But 2006 saw predicament weigh like a ton of bricks.

The club was relegated in bottom place having acquired a paltry twenty-four points from its thirty-eight matches, winning only five and conceding sixty-eight goals. The club immediately above them gained twelve points more: Cadiz, fellow Andalucians, where Malaga had capitulated 0-5 in the final match of that awful season. Meanwhile the president and biggest shareholder, Serafin Roldan, who'd taken over four years earlier upon Puche's departure, was looking to sell the debt-ridden club.

Alarmingly to anyone with the purest sporting principles at heart, one consortium reported to be interested in November 2005 was said to have close links with Arsenal; like Beveren of Belgium, Malaga would now become just a feeder club, merely servants of the destiny of another, a passport office for South Americans or Africans biding time for a higher stage. Malaga CF would be made financially secure through selling their right of self-determination. Thankfully, it never sank to that.

In the summer of 2006 the club got a new owner in the bulky shape of Lorenzo Sanz, the ex-president of Real Madrid whose son Fernando was already at La Rosaleda as centre-back and captain. Sanz paid six million euros to take control, took on the club's horrendous debt of thirty million, and installed Fernando – at the age of just thirty-two – as president. The Sanz family duly embarked upon sorely needed changes in the running of the club and unsurprisingly some measures were unpopular. As part of a huge economy drive, it was even proposed in September that some players and staff in the reserve team should work unpaid, and a strike was promptly threatened. Two months later Fernando Sanz announced that there was no alternative but to voluntarily appoint a legal administrator to restructure the debt now standing at twenty-eight million euros: a lengthy process.

It's easy for myself to say this, but it seems to me that Fernando Sanz deserves much credit. At one point his father had given him licence to quit, given the flak he was getting, but he'd insisted on seeing matters through. One of those matters he'd seen through had been the team's averting catastrophe. If the building of the new Tribuna Stand perhaps had been, in hindsight, a financial gamble at that time, then the 2006-7 season on the pitch might have brought financial disaster. With the higher waged players moved on, a depleted team struggled against further demotion, and salvation was achieved only in the penultimate match. Had the club sunk into the third division, it would surely have been the end.

Fernando Sanz had also, meanwhile, overseen the appointment of a new coach who'd joined from UD Marbella back in October. This new man was Juan Ramon Lopez Muniz, a disciple of and former assistant to Juande Ramos of Sevilla fame when the latter had coached Malaga in the 2003-4 season. In the past close-season Muniz had brought in no fewer than eleven new players – nine 'bargain buys' and two loanees – and a similar number exited. With such wholesale change, the coach could now look upon the team as one of his own making. All he had to do now was get it to play. He hadn't made a bad start to this 2007-8 campaign: Malaga had won their first two league games, at home to Salamanca and away at Alaves, and three days prior to this Cordoba match they'd also knocked Celta de Vigo out of the Spanish Cup. Maybe things were looking up.

O O O

La Rosaleda was filling up, though nowhere near to capacity: whatever that was. *Marca*, a daily sports (mostly football) newspaper, had stated in its glossy guide to this new season that the capacity was 22,800. Others had put it appreciably higher at 34,000. It looked nearer that latter figure to me. La Rosaleda was also loudening up.

Away to my left, at the bottom of that end, a large group who'd determinedly spend the entire proceedings on their feet was kicking up a choral din, flags and banners aflight. Opposite them was a similar scene, one banner there proclaiming that Antonio Banderas was a *Malaguista* (which indeed he is). Above both groupings, of those who weren't sporting Malaga's blue and white stripes, most seemed to be wearing no shirt at all as the sun seared. There was – and would remain – a thundering drum somewhere. But the most vociferous lot of all, standing on high and just to the right of the Preferencia Stand across the pitch from me, were the *Malaka Hinchas*, Malaga CF's major mob of exhortation, dutifully recalling the city's original name given it by the founding Phoenicians. On the fringe of the *Hinchas* I could see a flag with three lions in its top left corner. The *Pena Internacional Malaguista*, created by expats eight years earlier in Marbella, was by now an officially recognised supporters' club, and around two thousand – mainly British – expats now held Malaga CF season tickets. Those English opposite were evidently committed: like myself, they'd come here this evening instead of watching England play Israel in a Euro 2008 qualifier 'live' on television.

It wasn't only the home fans who were warming up. To my right, in a corner of the upper tier, was the travelling Cordoba contingent. Something I've forever found baffling about Spanish football fans is that, unlike in England, and except for cup finals or particularly crucial matches, they barely seem to do just that: travel. Maybe the culture is indeed one of just defending your *pueblo* without needing to invade that of others (unless perhaps you're a Real or Barca fan watching your club once a season in your hometown stadium). Yet some fans do feel the need to follow their team, so I still wonder why more don't. Cordoba isn't so far from Malaga, but I estimated their following to be around only a couple of hundred. Fair play to these, though: the *Brigadas Blanquiverdas* were all announcing themselves now.

As the evening unfolded, matters off the pitch would engage me most of all.

○ ○ ○

The pitch itself wasn't in best condition. In years gone by the legendary likes of Ricardo Zamora, Helenio Herrera and Ladislao Kubala had sat alongside it as CD Malaga's coach, and Juanito had bestrode it in the late 1980s after his stellar years at Real Madrid, but a month ago it'd staged a pop concert and taken a real battering. Sections of it had subsequently undergone returfing, but still it looked messy – rather like this match today, in which no individual would catch the eye as being better than ordinary. Two absentees through injury, both centre-forwards, were Malaga's Salva Ballesta who'd won the *Pichichi* in 2000 when with Racing de Santander, and Cordoba's Javi Moreno who'd scored twice in three minutes in the 2001 UEFA Cup Final when Alaves bravely were edged by Liverpool.

Malaga, with so many new faces, were naturally still in the process of bedding in and so a lack of cohesion on their part today was entirely understandable. For their own part, Cordoba had only just clawed their way out of the third division. Fifteen thousand watched, then, this somewhat untidy affair of too many unforced errors, the poor quality typified not only by wayward passes and heavy touches but also by lack of intelligent movement. And while Muniz would have been horrified by the visitors' 22nd-minute equaliser when Pineda was allowed to turn and cross from the left for Cristian Alvarez, unmarked at the back post, to put away the header, Cordoba's coach Paco Jemez would have been similarly appalled on the hour by Baha's totally free header in front of goal.

That goal by Baha was Malaga's demoralising fourth, just three minutes after their third, but until this quick-fire double the contest had actually been quite even. Malaga's first goal, on sixteen minutes, had been the game's most spectacular, an explosive thirty-yard free-kick by their Brazilian-born left-back Rossato, which Cordoba's veteran goalkeeper (Julio Iglesias!) even so should have dealt with. The lead had been regained four minutes before the break by a twenty-yard low potshot from the Portuguese centre-back Helder Rosario, and added to when ex-Barca junior Antonio Hidalgo, who would also provide the cross for Baha's fourth, ran through unopposed from central midfield to slot home.

It wasn't an ill-tempered match (though Cordoba's centre-back Pablo Ruiz became rather feisty towards the end and, having first been cautioned, got sent off), and nor were there any really bad tackles (though, pleasingly without this being any diving show, knocks were occasionally 'emphasised' by their recipients), but the referee somehow saw fit to issue eight yellow cards and two reds: one of the latter, for dissent, to no less a figure than Paco Jemez. This, after half an hour, provided the evening's most farcical moment when, thus banished to the stands, Jemez chose the gymnastic route by clambering over the fencing. If the referee, a sort of Extremaduran Uriah Rennie named Ceballos Silva, pompous but poor and basically from another planet, wasn't enamoured by this mickey-taking, nor would he have been best pleased by his subsequent *Marca* rating: zero. In truth, *Marca* uses a somewhat imprecise scale of nought to three; and, for the record, of the twenty-seven players rated for their performances at La Rosaleda, nineteen received just one, only five were awarded two, and three, including Julio Iglesias, like the ref, got zilch. Despite the fact that, between them, they'd provided five goals.

○ ○ ○

If Paco Jemez had acted eccentrically, then there was a wonderfully similar episode five minutes after Malaga's fourth goal.

Those *Hinchas* kicked up a virtually continuous racket, but should they pause for breath then they'd immediately be whipped up again by the groups behind the goals, fed by them, especially those fans to my left who were virtually forever at it themselves, and quite often most of the rest would join in as well. From the *Brigadas Blanquiverdas*, too, would come thunderclaps. Fair play indeed to these Cordoba fans. Just after their team had gone 1-4 down, they bellowed particularly vigorously; and such a show of loyalty drew genuine applause from the *Malaguistas*, which in turn provoked each set of supporters to then chant the other team's name, before everyone launched into some mutually engaging Andalucian ditty. A derby, yes, but there was respect and kinship about it: heartwarming stuff. But my cockles were warmed no more so than after sixty-five minutes. Some character emerged from among the *Hinchas* carrying a massive blue and white flag and proceeded, stopping in turn in front of each section, to run the entire length of the Preferencia Stand wielding it, stirring up those fans still more and rousing the whole lot around La Rosaleda. His egged-on return run brought the same, then he disappeared back whence he'd sprung to a roar of re-embrace and another reverberating din of support.

Towards the end of the game there was a mass-celebratory, Argentinian-style, feet-bouncing boing all around the place; even the Cordoba lot engaged themselves in it. To myself, that seemed the icing on the cake of this mightily refreshing rumbustiousness which I'd encountered here. Prawn-sandwiched Old Trafford, old Highbury library, all the mute rest of them, this wasn't. Raw vitality, this was.

○ ○ ○

The temperature was still twenty-four degrees as I departed, past the beer stalls where fans mixed, revelling car horns amid the cacophony, dangling *Malaguista* flags amid the gridlock. As I made my way back towards the train station, I reflected on what I'd just seen. Though the standard of football hadn't been good, the overall experience had been an uplifting one, the atmosphere brimming and the support truly marvellous, stewards (and indeed police) barely in evidence either, any plainclothed stewards that there were just on hand to point towards your seat, no bumptious jobsworths in orange anoraks eyeing you as prey. Football fans had been trusted and allowed to give full vent to their emotions, and no-one had crossed any line. Christ, that took me back.

Back in Fuengirola, I called into Bar Everest, run by Cristobal, to catch the last half-hour of Spain's struggling 1–1 draw in Reykjavik, part of their struggle to qualify for Euro 2008. Cristobal chunters a lot, is a touch batty, and mad-keen on Real Madrid, his walls festooned with *Madridista* paraphernalia, pride of place given to a huge ornamental boot presented to him by Fuengirola-born Juanito. Back in June, after Real had clinched the league title, Bar Everest had been boisterously chock-full, but now there was only a handful, and silent at that. "Always problem....every time...." said Cristobal matter-of-factly, and nor did anyone then show much emotion when Iniesta equalised with four minutes to go. Certainly not two nearby old women sat nattering outside their open front doors on white plastic chairs evidently borrowed from the bar, even though it was knocking midnight by now.

But I gazed at this little dimly lit street scene, and at Cristobal's photographs as he started, jabbering again, to clear away, then remembered something Graham Hunter had once said on television in the days when I'd had to content myself in Birmingham with Sky's coverage of Spanish football, wishing I were there: '....to rediscover a love of football, which was one of the reasons I came to Spain....'

Well, here I was myself now; and, for better or worse, I'd made a start.

-2-
PERSPECTIVE
Tuesday 25ᵗʰ September

To many folk, the thought of living on the Costa del Sol would be an idyllic one. Maybe owning a bar there, playing 'mine host', enjoying a leisurely lager with regulars as the sun beats down upon the glittering Med before going home to your nice house in the hills, perhaps a dip in your pool in the small hours. But, in all too many cases that I quickly became aware of, the reality is very different. Living on the Costa del Sol can be a real bitch of a struggle, as businesses strive to make ends meet and people work all hours, sometimes in two jobs, to pay the rent. Frank the Manc with his bar on Fuengirola's front had been feeling the pinch as he competed for custom on a coastline that was forever sprouting new development and wider choice. One day back in June he'd actually said to me, "It's soul-destroying." This coming from a determined man of cheery disposition and, ex-Army, hard as nails. Myself, I felt fortunate. I'd taken early retirement, had a pension, a few bob in the bank too, and no mortgage around my neck.

Until recently, someone in particular not far away had doubtless felt fortunate too, and many folk would have considered him to be living an idyllic life.

Then fate struck. At least Frank's still around to battle on, while I'm still around to explore. Maybe Frank will turn his corner, and maybe I'll take a wrong turn, but, whatever, we'd both still be able to look at the blue sky and feel the sunshine: we'd both be alive. Every now and again, something happens to somebody else that gives perspective, and shows how preciously fragile everything can be.

As a kid, Antonio Puerta had been a big fan of Sevilla. He was also blessed with a talent that enabled him to get to play for them, which is dreamy enough, but he was also playing for them in their most successful era ever. He'd recently also broken into the national squad. On Saturday 25th August, Sevilla had kicked off a new season rich in further promise at home to Getafe. Thirty minutes into the game, Puerta collapsed. Three days later, three months short of his twenty-third birthday, he was dead. Within two months, he would have become a father for the first time.

○ ○ ○

I'd developed something of a soft spot for Sevilla, for quite a few reasons. For one, under Juande Ramos, I'd liked watching them play on television. The ironic thing here is that my own preferred style of play puts a premium on ball possession: if you've got the ball, the other team can't hurt you, and patiently you can hurt them. But I'd looked at Ramos' Sevilla and found them a breath of fresh air. Not that Sevilla cheerfully squandered possession themselves – far from it. But they played with real gusto and conviction: forceful, fast, fluent, using the width of the pitch, getting numbers up quickly in support, forever positive, taking risks. They'd seemed to say: we'll score more than you. They'd looked so strong, so swarming, so throttling, with a stamina quite awesome. They were exciting to the senses.

They also had Enzo Maresca who'd played thirty-odd games for The Baggies while a teenager, still fondly remembered in those parts as a real talent who gave his all and managed to grin through it too. But there's something else: an image I can still see now. When Sevilla faced Middlesbrough in Eindhoven for the 2006 UEFA Cup (Enzo scoring twice in a comprehensive 4-0 demolition), the television camera had picked out a middle-aged chap among the Spanish horde at one end, and several times returned to pick him out again. In that chap, any real football fan would have seen himself: love in his heart, misery burnt into him over all the years, anxiety etched on his face, eyes fearful, yet still hope in his soul, especially tonight, a thousand please Gods, we've won nothing in my lifetime, please God just this once, here, now, tonight. When Sevilla's victory became inevitable, there were tears rolling. His mates hugged him, one seemed playfully to rib him for being such a big softie, and I loved him for being what he was.

o o o

The train journey from Malaga to Seville, mountainously picturesque at first but then rather featureless, took two and a half hours but should have taken much less than that, like a bus driver content just to trundle along in second gear. Again, I hadn't the foggiest idea where the stadium was, so I took a cab from Santa Justa station: for less than a mile. The driver had given me a look. Given the proximity of the Estadio Ramon Sanchez Pizjuan, I'd thought he'd considered me stupid, lazy or both, but then the real reason came to light. "*Te gusta Sevilla?*" I'd asked ("Do you like Sevilla?") as he fiddled for my change. As soon as I'd put the question, I'd wondered if he knew I meant of course not the city itself but one of its football teams. "No," said he without looking up. Then, having turned to face me, and emphasising his last word with a sardonic smile: "I am Betis." Well, it was a bit of a naff enquiry.

It was only half-one, kick-off wasn't until nine o'clock, but I wanted to make sure of a ticket.

Some would consider much of graffiti to be quite artistic. I'm certainly no art expert, but to me art should deliver a state of grace, and graffiti on public walls delivers to me only a defacing eyesore, however intricate and colourful it might be, plus there's something sadly sneaky about it. But what I saw this afternoon was above that. The wall housing the ticket windows had become some concrete book of remembrance and there were literally hundreds of entries, many from Betis fans, this in a city where its two football clubs especially polarised commitment.

Puerta had been running back to help snuff out any Getafe danger when he collapsed, close to his goalmouth, with no-one else around him. Andres Palop, the goalkeeper, had immediately realised. The summoned help had eventually resuscitated him, Puerta had eventually sat up on his haunches, barely of this world, and he'd actually walked off, down the steps too towards the changing-rooms. He'd had a history of this sort of thing, had fainted twice in recent months, but tests had determined nothing. Now, though, this insidious heart attack was persistent and wouldn't be denied. Three nights later I'd watched live on television the scene at the Sanchez Pizjuan, a part of it now both place of rest and chapel. It was knocking three in the morning and there were hundreds, perhaps thousands, there in respect, more than a few in Betis' green and white stripes. Sevilla had been due to play a Champions League qualifier in Athens that same night, had flown straight back without kicking a ball, and the bus had now arrived home, team-mates making a beeline. There was inevitably subdued applause at first, but then a cathartic crescendo of 'Sevilla!! Sevilla!!' It was genuinely moving.

Ticket ensured, I now had to find digs for two nights' stay. When I'd moved to Spain there'd been so many things, football aside, that I wanted to do, special places to experience. I'd been here all of this time, albeit through a burning and lethargy-inducing summer, but still I'd never been to romantic Seville, the quintessential city of Andalucia, synonymous with possibly the most moving form of the blues – flamenco – and one of the more moving of dramas – *Carmen*. I was going to spend a couple of days here at last; if only I could find a hotel room in this tourists' magnet. The convenient Novotel, like so many, was full, so I traipsed, and then traipsed some more. Eventually I was pointed in the direction of Casa Araceli, a private residence of several floors in the throes of hotel conversion, run by a septuagenarian Frenchwoman who was at least two tomatoes short of the proverbial, though not so naive: sixty euros a night for a room whose television was without remote control, whose sink was out of order, where the shared bathroom was without shower curtain, and where the flushing of toilet paper was discouraged in favour of a stomach-churning bin. Bless her. She'd lovingly prepare me a special breakfast, atop plate and flanked by knife and fork, of a solitary peach. But the room was in the ancient and atmospheric Santa Cruz quarter with its narrow, twisting alleyways, and very close to the particularly historical – and beautiful – sites and sights. So I was now embedded. But tomorrow's tourism could wait.

Andalucia delights in letting you know how hot it is and so, as I sauntered around in the early evening, the neon sign told me it was not only half-six but also thirty-seven degrees. This had naturally demanded regular water intake between the odd lager and fortifying *tapas*, the latter especially fortifying if they involve potatoes, arguably Spain's most popular discovery in the New World. I edged closer towards the stadium and now the match was in the air, Sevilla shirts becoming more numerous. Somehow I recalled Guillem Balague's words of a year earlier as I'd sat at home in the West Midlands: 'Seville is a city that lives, eats and breathes football! And Sevilla and Betis hate each other!' I'd wondered whether Sky's Balague would be here on this Tuesday evening, for his beloved Espanyol were the visitors. In my limited knowledge till now of football in this city, one thing I'd wholly admired was that such rabidness of support had persisted despite a virtual absence of triumph: prior to 2005, Sevilla and Betis had won only six trophies (one league title each) between them.

How the rivalry had begun was rather quirky. Real Betis Balompie had come about through a merger, but one of those merging clubs had itself earlier come about, in 1909, through a split within the ranks at Sevilla (rather like Liverpool's materialisation out of Everton). But whereas the Merseyside rivalry has been largely quite fraternal over the years, despite Liverpool's going on to achieve roaring success that put the blue half of that city much in their shade, the Seville rivalry has been anything but brotherly love. If the very first derby encounter back in 1915 had sunk into violence involving both players and fans, then more recent events had underlined the ongoing antipathy. In 1995 Sevilla's president and Betis' chief executive had swapped punches during a radio show; in 2002 the Sanchez Pizjuan was shut for four games following derby rioting; and just seven months ago a Spanish Cup quarter-final second-leg match between the two at Betis' home had been abandoned after fifty-six minutes when Juande Ramos was knocked unconscious by a half-full bottle. That latter incident provoked the Spanish federation to look into the antics of both clubs' presidents whom it accused of forever fomenting the bad blood. A couple of years earlier Jose Maria del Nido, president of Sevilla, who once declared himself to be 'the most important man in Seville except for the Pope', had delighted in pointedly stating how wonderfully historic it would be for the city to achieve a place in the UEFA Champions League; at the time he'd said that, of course, Sevilla were almost certain to do exactly that. But Sevilla then contrived to snatch disaster from the jaws of triumph and, against all odds, it was Betis instead who grabbed that place on the very last day of the season, prompting their vocal chief executive Manuel Ruiz de Lopera to gloat (and, boy, did their partying fans gloat too): 'He's right. This is historic.' The bitter pill that Sevilla were forced to swallow was made all the more acrid by Betis' winning of the Spanish Cup that season too, but since then the force had been with themselves. Whilst Betis had struggled in the bottom half of the table (only escaping relegation in 2007 by winning their final game in Santander), Sevilla, upon appointing Ramos as their coach in the summer of 2005 to succeed the more defensive-minded Joaquin Caparros, had roared their way to a flurry of trophies. After thrashing Middlesbrough, they'd vibrantly dismantled Barcelona 3-0 in Monaco to lift the UEFA Supercup, they'd defeated Espanyol at Hampden Park to retain the UEFA Cup, and they'd beaten Getafe three months ago to win the Spanish Cup, the latter triumph bringing their first domestic trophy in fifty-nine years. Then they'd thrashed Real Madrid 5-3 in the Bernabeu one month ago to take the Spanish Supercup too.

Whilst del Nido, a lawyer by profession, had all too often indulged in bluster, the club now had a clearly structured modus operandi. With a budget roughly at best a fifth the size of Barcelona's and a seventh that of Real Madrid, Sevilla had plotted their progress by means of a fertile youth development system, a global scouting network, value for prudent money in the transfer market; and latterly Juande Ramos' unshakeable belief in his playing method, fast-and-furious for ninety minutes. Over recent years that youth scheme had produced the likes of Carlos Marchena, Jose Antonio Reyes and Sergio Ramos, had provided over twenty first-teamers in less than a decade, and since 1997 had reaped in excess of fifty million pounds in sales. The scouting system had brought in the likes of the Brazilian Daniel Alves from Bahia for merely half a million pounds. Julio Baptista, meanwhile, was snapped up in 2003 from Sao Paulo for two million pounds, was converted from a midfielder into a prolific forward, then sold within two years to Real Madrid for £13 million. And whilst Juventus had paid Albion five million pounds for Enzo Maresca in 2000, Sevilla had snapped him up five years later – still aged only twenty-five – from Fiorentina for just two million pounds, having seen how much he still had to offer. Although Sevilla had been sellers – Reyes, Ramos and Baptista prime examples – it'd been the bringing in, that seeing of how much certain players had to offer, which had been key to the team's recent phenomenal success. Monchi, the sporting director, and Juande Ramos had seen hunger as crucial: any incoming players had to possess burning ambition to achieve. In that way, and convinced of his approach, they'd take on board Ramos' demands of them, and bond together.

From being a club that was £30 million in debt when del Nido assumed the presidency in 2002, Sevilla had now themselves qualified for the UEFA Champions League, winning those five trophies along the way. And they might have done even more. In 2006 they'd finished fifth, but only two points behind runners-up Real Madrid, whilst in 2007, having been serious title contenders throughout the season, they'd eventually finished third, just lacking that killer touch to capitalise upon Real's and Barca's falterings. But Sevilla, like Deportivo and Valencia had proved by winning the championship in recent years, like Real Sociedad who'd thrown the title away four years ago, had shown that the 'Big Two' weren't padlocked into supremacy.

That said, Sevilla's shirt had now begun to show a few pulled stitches. Monchi had said that players joining the club were determined to put themselves on the map, and two who'd done just that had recently been looking further afield. Alves, the scintillating attacking right-back, had welcomed being courted by Chelsea and Real Madrid during the close-season – 'Mercenario', screamed a banner inside the Sanchez Pizjuan at the Getafe game – while Frederic Kanoute, reborn since moving to Andalucia and scorer of twenty-one goals in thirty-two league games in the 2006-7 season, had been in constant touch with his agent over the summer. Not only that but Ramos himself – who'd made no secret of his being open to job offers elsewhere, nor of his liking for the English Premiership – had very recently met with Tottenham officials in a Seville hotel. Such machinations hadn't prevented the team from subsequently demolishing Real Madrid (Kanoute hitting a hat-trick), nor from overturning an early deficit to beat Getafe 4-1. But, whether or not due to an unsettled air about the place, or whether or not the Antonio Puerta tragedy had impacted harmfully, the juggernaut had begun to splutter. AC Milan had beaten them 3-1 in Monaco for the UEFA Supercup on August 31st and, whilst they'd also beaten Recreativo de Huelva 4-1 at the Sanchez Pizjuan in the league, they'd lost 0-3 at Arsenal in the UEFA Champions League six days ago and then again 1-2 at Barcelona in the league three days ago. I'd watched these last two games on television. At the Emirates Stadium they'd of course played positively but Arsenal, quite frankly, were awesome. There'd also been two moments in that game when Sevilla had irked me: Arsenal's first goal had come about through Escude's turning his back to Fabregas' shot, deflecting it past Palop, and in the second half Alves had gestured for Clichy to be given a yellow card, waving an oh-so-distasteful imaginary one at the Swedish referee, who rightly then gave Alves himself a real one. In Barcelona, Sevilla had been less positive than usual in a bitty goalless first half, and in the second, though wearing their pink strip for the Camp Nou's fiftieth birthday match, they'd been a pale shadow, totally dominated, pinned back, and Kanoute's last-minute goal as the clock approached midnight had distorted the scoreline.

But that soft spot of mine for this team was still there and, in tonight's rematch of that UEFA Cup Final staged in Glasgow back in May, I was looking for Sevilla – never mind that I was sweltering right now – to warm the cockles of my heart again.

○ ○ ○

Not that I had anything against Espanyol. And whilst I suspect that some folk might look kindly upon them out of sympathy, or even contrariness, due to their being forever a virtual afterthought in the shadow of their illustrious city neighbours, those folk might be surprised by a particular statistic (and how the Spanish print media, quite mind-bogglingly, love their statistics!). Espanyol, historically, is ranked the sixth most successful club in Spain, above the likes of both Seville clubs, Zaragoza and Real Sociedad. Whilst they'd won just four trophies – all of those being Spanish Cups, the last two as recently as 2000 and 2006 – their ranking reflects the fact that they'd only ever spent four seasons out of the top flight. Along the way, they'd provided forty players for the Spanish national team and they'd also managed to reach two UEFA Cup Finals, both lost only through penalty shoot-outs. All of this, to my mind, constitutes a record to be rather proud of. Espanyol was also one of the first clubs in Spain to be formed exclusively by Spaniards as opposed to expatriates, and they'd also inflicted upon Real Madrid the heaviest defeat in their history, 1-8, albeit way back in March 1930. The fabled goalkeeper Ricardo Zamora had started out with Espanyol, and others who'd worn their shirt over the years included, though in his twilight years, Alfredo di Stefano himself.

Their current squad contained some tasty players too, none more so than their talismanic captain and centre-forward, Raul Tamudo, who'd effectively cost Barca the previous season's championship with a last-gasp equaliser at the Camp Nou in the penultimate match. Add the sureness tonight that Espanyol would be seeking revenge – a powerful motivator in football – for their cruel defeat at Hampden, when they'd played fifty minutes with ten men and were denied only on penalties, and I was now licking my lips in anticipation of not only some *patatas bravas* but also a spicy football match.

○ ○ ○

I hadn't taken too much note of the Sanchez Pizjuan upon my first glimpse of it, making straight for the ticket windows but then being captivated by the Antonio Puerta tributes, yet I'd still been struck by its size; it looked, in fact, formidable, a huge edifice of concrete that once had held 70,000. Now, as I made for it a second time, and at the risk of stating the obvious, I simply said to myself: this is a football stadium. True, there was the large Nervion shopping mall not much more than spitting distance away, but there were none of those ugly steel girders so requisitely dominant in so many of those new or renovated English stadia, and nor were there those vast swathes of fortified glass that make you wonder if you're entering some office block. And then there was the marvellous mosaic at the main entrance: stretching twenty-five yards wide and reaching to virtually the full height of the stand, it featured the club's crest at its centre plus, flanking that, the crests of sixty clubs from Spain and around the globe who'd played here. This was a football stadium, and an imposing one. And I was able to make some comparisons because this wasn't actually the first top-division ground I'd been to since moving to Spain. Within two days of my arrival I'd set out for Barcelona for the Andorra-England match, and thus visited both the Olympic Stadium and the Camp Nou. Whilst the latter on my tour of it was, well, grand, I'd thought Espanyol's current home not impressive at all, certainly when I'd recalled other Olympic stadia I'd been to such as those in Berlin, Munich and Athens, and I'd also thought its innards to be musty and gloomy. That said, Espanyol currently had a new home, west of their city, under construction.

Now, for fifty-five euros (yes, I treated myself again, and nor do I have any problem with comfort when I'm neutral), I sat towards the top of the main Preferencia Stand, left of the halfway line. The vast majority inside the now 45,500-capacity, two-tiered bowl were at the mercy of the weather, but above me stretched a particularly distinguishing feature of the Sanchez Pizjuan, a roof of reddish steel design that curved curiously and gracefully upward but extended to cover the upper tier. It gave the place added dignity. Again, though, as at La Rosaleda, I thought how steep everywhere seemed, half-expecting someone here to topple out from one of those upper tiers behind the goals. And again, as at La Rosaleda, I thumbed through a free match programme. This one's centre spread showed a crowd scene from the previous home game, featuring a huge Puerta banner that had been unfurled, one which captured him in a famous and enduring pose: kissing his left hand after scoring the goal against Schalke in this stadium that sent Sevilla into their first UEFA Cup Final. Gazing around, I cast my mind back to other moments that the Sanchez Pizjuan had held, and recalled two events in particular. This was where Toni Schumacher had infamously flattened Patrick Battiston during an epic World Cup semi-final in 1982 between West Germany and France, and this was also where, four years later, Terry Venables' Barca had lost a European Cup Final against Steaua Bucharest. Prior to kick-off tonight, there'd be a particularly poignant moment. It was virtually a full house that watched the Espanyol players jog over to the spot and then lay a bouquet behind the byeline, a month now to the day since Puerta was struck: a solemn act that drew warm appreciation.

The crowd then proceeded to demonstrate just how hot they were, and I'm not talking now about the air temperature. In coming to live in Spain and experience its football, one thing I'd wondered about was the matchday experience itself: in particular, how much passion might be generated in the stands? Two and a half weeks earlier the Malaga crowd had given me a real glow inside. Now, in Seville, this was pulsating stuff (little wonder that the Spanish federation had often sent the national team to play here over the years). The boisterous support was almost incessant and occasionally Sevilla's main mob – the *Biris* gathered in the lower tier of the north stand to my left – would blast out some special chorus whose opening burst was a genuine shock to the eardrums. In those moments were thoughts of anything else obliterated. Much of being a football fan is to do with escapism, with being transported into a different consciousness where the soul's left the everyday body behind. I wasn't feeling as passionate as these *Biris*, nor as fearful as that good old boy in Eindhoven, but I'd been transported by them all. And I'll be totally honest now, even though I feel quite guilty in admitting it. Albion were playing Cardiff City this same night in a League Cup game at The Hawthorns. I received a text message that told me we were being stuffed. I felt grateful to these folk here for snatching my woes, ripping them up, and tossing them into the Andalucian night. Plus, a ripping yarn was unfolding on the pitch, although it didn't get really going till after half-time. In the meantime, despite a young kid's wearing of a Maresca shirt a few rows in front that tried to distract me, and once more being able to smile at the beer-swilling going on around me unaborted by any anoraks, and of course enjoying my concentration-enhancing smokes, the first half had thrown up two gems.

The first was one of pure charm, albeit born of sorrow. It'd taken me a few seconds to realise, wondering why. Then I'd looked at the clock, and also somehow half-twigged that this might have been his shirt number. After sixteen minutes, for the whole of the next one, the Sanchez Pizjuan fell absolutely silent.

Thirteen minutes later, respect duly having given way at kick-off to affairs of state, with Espanyol displaying splendid organisation in the face of Sevilla's mere spluttering, the visitors took the lead. The gem was in the finish. Angel had been allowed to find himself all alone just inside the box although, as pressure materialised, swiftly but too late, he opted to shoot early. Among a myriad of irritations back in England, and where football itself was concerned, had been some hypertensive black BBC man, or some weary-voiced Sky Ulsterman, or some Glaswegian self-styled voice of Sky authority (and never mind that all three had turned out for The Baggies), forever trying to tell me that the overriding necessity is to – just – 'hit the target'. Well, leaving out of the argument that I'd never used to hear that now hackneyed expression – neither Kenneth Wolstenholme nor knowledgeable ex-pros like Walley Barnes had ever mouthed it – I'm personally not having it. Yes, I understand some of the reasoning: the goalkeeper might spill the ball, or you might earn a corner-kick. But good players don't just 'hit the target' or 'work the goalkeeper'. They try to beat the goalkeeper so that the ball finishes up in the net. Sometimes they might aim for the top corner and narrowly miss; is such an attempt really worse than some hit-and-hope bumble 'on target'? Angel arrowed the ball expertly an inch inside Palop's left post.

O O O

In the second half the contest took off, especially given that Espanyol doubled their lead after nine minutes of it. During the break Juande Ramos had made two changes, one of those substituted being the Colombian centre-back Mosquera by the Ivorian striker Arouna Kone, but Ramos' choice to fill in at the back had surprised me: Enzo. In my memory he'd never been the quickest, nor the most athletic on the turn, and now Albert Riera (one goal in nineteen appearances for Manchester City two seasons earlier) left him behind for Luis Garcia to very neatly convert his low cross at the near post.

What was going on? Were normally explosive Sevilla going to lose yet again? And at home? To an unheralded team like Espanyol?

To a good team for whom what had happened in Glasgow still rankled?

But now Sevilla began to look much more like their normal selves, really forcing the play, although they needed a stroke of good fortune to reduce the deficit. On the hour Jesus Navas drove a low ball from the right into the goalmouth, where Jarque deflected it into his own net. Ramos then turned up the heat by bringing on Kanoute for the left-back Adriano – with a demanding schedule that involved another Champions League fixture in seven days' time, he'd been engaging in squad rotation – so that Sevilla now had three natural strikers on the pitch. And after sixty-eight minutes Kone, for whom the club had forked out all of twelve million euros to PSV Eindhoven a month earlier, looped home a header from a cross by the pugnacious young left-winger Diego Capel, the other half-time substitute for ex-Malaga midfielder Duda.

Surely, I thought, Sevilla would go on and win it now. The team was firing (though not their Russian striker Kerzhakov who'd already fluffed two gilt-edged chances) and the *Biris*, especially, were pumping up the volume. Good on the *Biris*: they'd created a hell of a din of support immediately after Luis Garcia's goal. But shortly after Kone's equaliser two things happened that would ultimately conspire to puncture Sevilla's ascendancy. Maresca damaged his groin, and Espanyol brought on Raul Tamudo. Sevilla's storming forward – and indeed their offensive formation – was leaving them somewhat susceptible to counter-attacks, and Maresca's reduced mobility was accentuating the threat.

Two minutes from the end, totally against the run of play and in the face of all expectation inside the Sanchez Pizjuan (I couldn't see any visiting fans), Espanyol plundered the winner. Sevilla had been found threadbare on their left, from where Angel put a low ball infield which Maresca failed to cut out. It reached Tamudo, now in through the middle alone on Palop. Once more the finish was expert, the ball drilled home an inch inside the goalkeeper's right post. At which point the *Biris* struck up again: and kept it going to the bitter end, when there were no boos or whistles. Fantastic support.

So. Espanyol had exacted their revenge. Sevilla had suffered a rare home defeat – but also now their third loss in a row, the first time for two and a half years that they'd experienced such a depressing sequence, prompting questions in the press, all matters considered, of some mini-crisis.

And for myself?

Well, I'd experienced my first top-flight Spanish league game and, yes, a spicy offering it'd been too, an engaging contest full of good football performed by accomplished technicians at a lively tempo, all in front of a fervent crowd. I really couldn't have asked for much more. But also pleasing was that the match had been played in a fair spirit. I suspected that some form of sharp practice was bound to disgust me before too long, but inside the Sanchez Pizjuan tonight I'd noticed no real cynicism, whether diving or anything else. Nor had the referee been overly fussy. And, as at Malaga, there'd been no officiousness off the pitch either. I left the stadium, stopped to admire that mosaic again, then headed off into the night to look for my everyday body.

I'd surely been lucky so far. Two matches sampled and two heartening experiences. Yes, I recognised that the element of novelty had played a considerable role: that was an inevitable part of the something new I was treading, and maybe even a part of that something different I was seeking anyway, unacquainted surroundings enhancing the glow. But novelty's role had been much less than a leading one; the something different I'd felt inside so far hadn't relied on that, it'd been pure in its own right. Novelty, by definition, wears off in any case. I just hoped that this early glow wouldn't go the same way.

And speaking of glows, how even more wondrous Seville's cathedral – the biggest church in the world but much more than that – looked at midnight. Byron, who'd also spent time in my home city of Nottingham (nobody can accuse me of being a glory-hunter – and I'd fallen in love with Albion in the same season that Forest won the FA Cup), had once described Seville as 'a pleasant city, famous for oranges and women'. Taking those words merely at face value, you might be led to say today that Spain is a big country, famous for beaches and Real Madrid. Of course there's a bit more to it than that and, with Seville's oozing history, grandeur and romance, I'd wished I'd been able to soak up more of it on this, my first visit, the panorama from atop the Giralda tower heightening the allure. Unlike someone who'd helped put one of its football teams firmly on the map, though, I still had my chance to.

   — "*Sevilla o Betis?*" I enquired again upon being dropped off at Santa Justa.
   — "*Betis*!!"
Life goes on.

3

JUANITO'S ROOTS
Sunday 18ᵗʰ November

It was the first time I'd ever heard anyone use the f-word at a football match and it was a player who'd used it. I was aged about twelve at the time and, aside from my innocent young self, there were probably another fifty-odd gathered for a Midland League game at Grange Park between Long Eaton United and Denaby United, the air thus thin enough to hear the odd cursing on the pitch. I think it must have been Denaby's left-back who was on the ball and under pressure, but it was definitely an ex-Barnsley goalkeeper and gruff Yorkshireman named Harry Hough who audibly didn't want the ball played back to him. Inevitably his call was ignored and the underhit backpass struggled vaguely in the direction of the custodian as a Long Eaton forward bore down upon him. Hough just managed to get there first and booted the ball somewhere in the direction of Nottingham before his ageing legs crumpled beneath him. "Fuckin' 'ell!!" he'd bellowed. "You fuckin' prat!!"

Grange Park is quite synonymous with innocence where I'm concerned. I didn't pay the place too many visits but I can remember another time when I'd gone there with a lad a few years older than myself. He'd pointed to the bottom of the three or four steps and said, "I 'ad a jump down there a couple o' nights ago." I'd merely wondered what on earth he'd been doing there alone at night just practising his agility. Also, Grange Park in those long-ago days had its resident lunatic at one grassy end; in fact, all by himself, he actually formed that end, bedecked in blue-and-white scarf, leaping about all over the place, gurgling, retrieving stray balls and miskicking them back to anywhere but the goalmouth. He'd gone to the same school as I, albeit at least a couple of years above me, and hence I recognised him. I haven't a clue what happened to him, Goodrich, but as a youth he was surely some kind of embryonic mad genius. Someone had told him, prior to some maths exam, that you couldn't take logarithm tables in with you, you had to learn them all off-by-heart. Innocently, he'd believed it. The word then came that he hadn't half made a good fist of reciting a sizeable chunk before someone else'd had a kinder word.

'The half-time Bovril was better,' said the great Brian Clough, famously. Grange Park, aside from being a place where the not-quites or past-its of Nottingham Forest or Derby County might grind their playing careers to a halt, had also been variously a leg-up for hopefuls or a real stepping-stone. Among the hopefuls was a kid I'd been at junior school with, David Hardy, who was untouchable at the age of eleven and of whom I wouldn't hear again until, one day, I'd picked up a copy of *The Long Eaton Advertiser* to discover that he was now at it for Long Eaton United. I think he also had a trial for Notts County. But he didn't make it. There was, however, a lad named Gary Hamson who'd played for Long Eaton when aged just fifteen and subsequently made a career at Bramall Lane and Elland Road. Another was Jack Lewis who went on to play for Wales. I'm afraid that my own sole claim to fame in just my Long Eaton Sunday League days was merely a case of reflected glory. I'd played against GIC of Borrowash whose centre-forward was someone who went on to play for England: Peter Ward. I couldn't get near him, but then again nor would Ally Robertson a few years later when Brighton came to The Hawthorns one night and, mostly due to Ward, knocked Albion out of the League Cup.

The prettiest person ever to come out of Long Eaton town

was surely Swing Out Sister's Corinne Drewery. She may even
have been the most talented. But Brian Clough had gone to look
at Garry Birtles. It seems strange looking back now, but
wonderful too, to remember Birtles' being part of the Long Eaton
United line-up inside the *Advertiser*, alongside other names such
as Muir who could only ever dream of going on to win
European Cups or playing alongside Brooking and Barnes for
England.

Before too long, with my spending time in Fuengirola, it had
been pointed out to me that none other than Juanito had started
out right here.

Having sampled Malaga and Sevilla, it was now time to seek
out something less oak and more acorn.

○ ○ ○

And indeed more earthy too, as Reg might have told me. Reg
was a chap I'd used to work with and his interest in football was
almost wholly confined to non-League. Not for him a Joneses'
wearing of some Manchester United or Chelsea shirt, nor any
prattling on a Monday morning about the state of the game based
only upon the latest armchair spoonfeeding of the afternoon
before. Reg got off his arse and actually went to games, home and
very often away, in support of his local club, Stafford Rangers.
Even though my own team was a League one, I had much more
in common with Reg than most. We shared a despising of not
only couch-potato know-alls but also that brainwashing which
held that the Premier League was the be-all and end-all, as if
everything and everyone else just didn't matter. Stafford Rangers
– his *pueblo* – meant a hell of a lot to Reg, although in his
decency (and his contempt for the incorrigibles) he wouldn't
vocalise that too much. He just quietly got on with his real
supporting. The big difference between the pair of us was that I
felt both the misery and futility of it all. I'd lived through times

that had held genuine hopes of real achievement only to then see such hopes crushed for ever. Reg knew all along that Stafford Rangers, never champions of England like Albion nor FA Cup winners, would never even sniff at glory. He felt his own sort of misery along his way, but never futility. Whilst we'd share downcast Monday mornings, the concept of pointlessness was wholly absent for Reg. Because of that, I felt just a little envy but also a whole lot of admiration for him. He'd curse about the latest home defeat but that wouldn't prevent his loyally going to places like Northwich Victoria five days later.

But it wasn't just the *pueblo* element for Reg. He also rejoiced in the integrity of it all, a million miles away from Murdoch's and Scudamore's dubious big business world where multi-millionaires postured, dived, squealed and roasted, all catalogued 'celebrity'-fashion in *The Sun*. He'd go to little market towns, drink in little social clubs with opponents' supporters, stand on some railway sleeper at one end, and connect with the sheer – if very limited – toiling on the pitch, posturing and squealing somewhere else on another planet, rawboned honesty right here. That was Reg's football world, absolutely unfutile and down-to-earth. Limited, yes, but joy of a kind.

So now I sought, hopefully, some Spanish equivalent, a different sort of antidote to the game I'd left behind in England.

○ ○ ○

Well, at least Stafford Rangers had its own website, often visited by Reg even when office narks were about. I was now about to find out just how unstraightforward it'd be to discover exactly where and when Fuengirola would kick off. In the throes of which I'd find out that they weren't called just Fuengirola any more, either.

My first port of call was Scotty whose acquaintance I'd already made on my previous visits to this corner of the world.

Scott McGregor now runs a cafe-bar named Scoffers on the front but also has a tale or three to tell. One of those is quite poignant: a once-in-a-lifetime chance of playing at Wembley denied. He said he'd been a member of the Scotland schoolboys' team that, just in this one year, Sod's Law to the fore, with England's boys' match against West Germany now earmarked for that venue, had been diverted to Nottingham's City Ground instead. Scott had been a junior at Ibrox, tempted to Highbury where he'd been an understudy to Kenny Sansom, had subsequently married the daughter of an Arsenal coach, and eventually carved out a new life on the Costa del Sol where, whilst forever naturally in touch with The Gunners, he'd also turned out for Fuengirola until injuries forced him to give up. "We played on sand!" he'd told me, and he'd enjoyed it too, the ball kept on the deck at a non-furious pace, "the way I liked it". But he had another sad story to come out with. Several years ago Fuengirola had earned promotion but, in order to take up their place in the higher division, were required to upgrade their arena. According to Scott, the local council had refused to fork out and the club, instead of ascending the hierarchy, was punitively despatched further down it. The best players, their efforts thrown back in their faces, and beyond the club's budget now anyway, thus left, and Fuengirola's brush with progress had resulted only in a portrait of crushing regression. "It was such a big shame," lamented Scott, a man familiar indeed with disappointment. "They were all good players and good lads too."

Scott, however, was evidently none too familiar now with his former team's current location. It plied its trade in the *Tercera Division*, Spain's regionalised fourth level (the third level is also regionalised, making promotion from those levels a convoluted process), and fixture lists are not readily on tap, certainly not in *Marca* which prints merely results and league tables. Based on that, but otherwise totally unarmed with information since any websites had proved elusive, outdated, contradictory and fixtureless, I'd guessed that 'Fuengirola' would be at home one coming weekend and thus one Saturday, on a whim, I'd thought I'd go to see them play, though I hadn't known whether they'd be playing today or tomorrow. "Turn sharp left after the train station, walk up that road about half a mile, turn to the left at Barclays bank," said Scott, "and it's just there."

When I'd got there, in a built-up area of apartment blocks and cafe-bars, I'd come across some not-quite-finished, smart new sports and leisure complex. A tiny backless stand whose capacity was around six hundred skirted one side of a spanking new artificial grass pitch, complete with all white markings and goalnets ready. Three old men were playing lunchtime cards over beer in the warm sunshine. I stepped inside, walked through the largely vacant restaurant area to the bar, and asked the only man there what time the kick-off was. He told me that they'd already played that morning. On a Saturday morning? I thought only school teams played on Saturday mornings. "And they play at Santa Fe."

- "Not here?"
- "No, at Santa Fe."
- "Where is Santa Fe?"
- "In Los Boliches."

That night I visited D's Bar in Fuengirola. The barman there was Barry whom I'd come to know quite well, especially as he'd used to follow The Baggies home and away prior to emigrating seventeen years ago. I'd guessed that because he'd been over here now for such a length of time, and presently on the far side of Fuengirola towards Los Boliches, he'd be able to point me in the right direction for some future attempt.

- "Santa Fe? That's where Los Boliches play."
- "No, the bloke told me it's where Fuengirola play."
- "Look, I should bloody know, it's my neck of the woods, and I'm telling you – Fuengirola play at Elola!"
- "Well they can't do, not now anyway."

Barry, from Dudley and roughly the same age as myself, is a somewhat crusty character. He calls me – and word soon gets round on the expat circuit – 'The Dinosaur', because he thinks I'm buried in the past, unwilling to embrace twenty-first century football (I haven't told him about this book I'm writing) or music (I've asked him why just about every radio station round here plays so much sixties', seventies' and eighties' stuff). I then half-recall that I'd perhaps seen somewhere a club name of Fuengirola Los Boliches.

- "Maybe Fuengirola and Los Boliches have merged," I ventured.

- "Merged?!" exclaimed The Crusty One. "They're big rivals! They even came to blows once! You talk some bollocks, you do!"

○ ○ ○

Well, this bollocks-talking dinosaur had a bit between its teeth now, and it soon had something else to chew on. I came across *El Futbol de Fuengirola* by Francisco Martin Benitez, a vast tome of four hundred pages charting the local football scene from 1916 to 2001. My Spanish, though by now I'd picked up a fair smattering, wasn't exactly all-embracing, but that fascinating tome nevertheless managed to put me right on several counts. It also underlined to me just how little the local club – Union Deportiva Fuengirola Los Boliches – counted today in the consciousness of expats: or, indeed, it seemed to me, of barely anyone else either.

I stumbled upon another website that linked into another that told me UD Fuengirola Los Boliches were due to play Club Deportivo Vera at the Estadio Santa Fe on Sunday 18th November. All I needed to know now was the kick-off time. I found CD Vera's website. '*Hora sin determinar*': to be arranged. Still work to do.

One warm Wednesday I strolled along the sea front for half

an hour, turned left up Calle Gibraltar, crossed two busy main thoroughfares, and finally found myself on the Avenida de las Salinas: Santa Fe, at last. No-one was around, no doors or windows open, no fixture posters. None of the surrounding buildings carried any publicity.

Back in Fuengirola I did something I should really have tried in the first place: ask inside the town hall. "*Si, domingo, a las dos de la tarde.*" Two o'clock kick-off. I sought confirmation elsewhere, in the Casa de Cultura. "Twelve o'clock, midday."

Later that evening I popped into a little jewel of a bar inside Plaza Yate off backstreet Calle Cuesta. This square, intimate and tidy, overlooked by stylish old apartments, holds an excellent restaurant and discreet little bars, one of which, tucked into a corner, is the Pena Juanito: a treasure trove of photographs showing the town as it had been sixty-odd years ago, but more predominantly a profusion of football memorabilia – photos, posters, pennants relating to local clubs and especially to the Real Madrid of Fuengirola's famous son. The owner was chatting with three men sat on barstools and, when I asked about Sunday's game, they all seemed suitably impressed. "Is our team!" beamed the owner, grey-haired and in his fifties. But.... "If you come in here on Saturday night, we can tell you then the kick-off." So I called in again three nights later. I could hear the rattle of pool balls as I approached from the backstreet. Half a dozen men, including the owner, were all standing around the table. A huge Spanish flag had been stuck up beneath the TV. They were all half-cut. My enquiry was met by the owner's glazed look and a shrug of his shoulders. One of his mates, with rather a struggle, leaned over to consult *Marca*.

I watched Spain stuff Sweden three-nil, thus ensuring their qualification for Euro 2008, on Cristobal's TV in Bar Everest. The triumphal cries together with all the Real Madrid festoonery seemed to emphasise all the more how UD Fuengirola Los Boliches was hardly even an afterthought. In the crowded bar, though, Juanito's ornamental boot came into contact with my leant-back head, and I took that as a sign. I was going to get myself to Santa Fe for around eleven in the morning and take it from there.

○ ○ ○

Paco Martin's huge labour of love, that vast historical tome, has its foreword penned – and highly appreciatively too – by Antonio Tapia. Now bespectacled and with receding silver hair, Tapia was currently the coach of Granada 74 in Spain's second division, but old photographs in Martin's book show him looking more like someone, fashionably coiffured and moustached, who might perhaps have joined up with Midge Ure in Ultravox. Tapia, aside from spending many years as a high school PE instructor, has spent his lifetime so far in this part of the world's football. He'd played in midfield for Club Deportivo Fuengirola and later Atletico Malagueno, the latter club now known as Malaga CF. As a coach he'd performed wonders for both Malaga CF's second string and its first team, saving the latter from what had looked like certain relegation from the *Primera* in 2005, beginning that stint by inspiring victories over Sevilla and Atletico Madrid. In his foreword, Tapia expressed much fondness for a subject with which he heartily identified, for such were his own roots.

And an engaging book it is. Another photograph shows Juan Antonio Samaranch, at that time merely a national sports delegate, ceremoniously opening in 1967 CD Fuengirola's then new ground, Campo Municipal Elola, the site of the rebuilt complex I'd erroneously visited that earlier Saturday afternoon. Others show Elola's being used, watched by a large crowd of more than three thousand, by Spain's national squad for training prior to a World Cup qualifier against Greece at La Rosaleda in 1973, the overseeing coach being the legendary Ladislao Kubala.

Over the years, so Martin's book informs, CD Fuengirola had locked horns in the lower leagues with the likes of Atletico Malagueno, Recreativo de Huelva and UD Almeria, clubs now familiar with Spain's elite division. And of course there are innumerable references to *nuestro inolvidable paisano* – our unforgettable comrade – Juan Gomez Gonzalez: Juanito.

I really do find old photographs fascinating, especially when they're heavily pregnant. One of my more treasured shows a Notts schoolboys' team of the late 1950s with Jeff Astle on the front row. And here now was Juanito as a mere sprog squatting amid mud for a boys' team named Aspes, then for CD Fuengirola's boys' team. Yes, everyone famous begins somewhere, naturally so, but I do find it engaging to look back whence they sprang, mud and innocence, years unrolled, anonymity yet to be visited by stardom.

Juanito had made his debut for CD Fuengirola's first team on 8th December 1968 against Puerto Malagueno in the *Regional Preferente*, then part of Spain's fourth level. Some creative form-filling had been involved, for he was only fourteen years and twenty-eight days old. In August 1969 he'd moved on to no less than Atletico Madrid, where he'd progressed through the youth ranks before sadly suffering a serious leg injury on his first-team debut, still aged only seventeen, in a friendly against Benfica. Recuperation would be so difficult that at one point he'd considered packing it all in, but he'd resurrected his career at Burgos, helping them achieve promotion to the top division in 1976, before arriving at Real Madrid a year later. By the time he left the Bernabeu in 1987 to wind down his playing days with CD Malaga – whom he nevertheless inspired to the second division championship in the first of his two seasons there – Juanito had helped Real to five league titles, two Spanish Cups and two UEFA Cups, and along the way he won the *Pichichi* in the 1983-4 season. In thirty-four games for the national team, among which were appearances in the 1978 and 1982 World Cup finals, he scored eight goals. For Real, meanwhile, he'd averaged almost one goal in three games, of which there'd been almost 350 in total. In a veritable myriad of Real Madrid superstars, Juanito remains *inolvidable*. Even today, after seven minutes (his shirt number), fans inside the Bernabeu chant: '*Illa, Illa, Illa, Juanito Maravilla!!*' (Juanito The Wonder).

I saw him just once in the flesh, in March 1981, when he played a leading role in a 2-1 win against England, and indeed provided Jesus Zamora's winner with an astute angled pass, besides hitting the bar with a deflected shot himself. This victory was, in fact, historic: Spain's sole ever triumph at Wembley, in the days when such an achievement by visiting nations was still rare.

Not bad going for a little lad who'd once upon a time got himself all muddied up in Fuengirola.

○ ○ ○

By the time I stepped off the local train in Los Boliches at just after half-ten that Sunday morning, I knew, courtesy of Paco, a lot more. He'd given me a rich flavour of Fuengirola's football scene but also facts. I knew now, for example, that the sad episode referred to by Scott had occurred back in 1992. CD Fuengirola, with Antonio Tapia as their coach, had achieved promotion to Spain's third level two years earlier, had finished as high as eighth the following season, but their financial state (debts of nine million pesetas) had then caused them to be demoted disastrously two levels to the *Regional Preferente*. Around this chaotic time, too, as Tapia took up a new post as coach of CD Los Boliches, CD Fuengirola merged with two local minor clubs to form Union Deportiva Fuengirola: the end of an era (and of a historic badge). Since then they'd alternated between the fifth and fourth levels. Along the way, in 2001, the ultimate fusion had been brought about: the end of thirty-odd years' rivalry with the relatively new kids on the block (CD Los Boliches hadn't come into being till 1973), and another new badge to emblemise that, however hard to wear for many. For I couldn't help thinking, as I'd ploughed through Paco Martin's work, that Fuengirola and its fans had looked upon themselves as elder statesmen in comparison with Los Boliches' upstarts. That rivalry had indeed occasionally been less than healthy. Whilst a few Fuengirola fans might ultimately have crawled over their thresholds after making their sorrows-drowning way back from Santa Fe in March 1987 following a 1-9 hammering, then nine years later at Elola came those blows of which Barry must have been thinking. Fuengirola won 1-0 in a match of two sendings-off, the referee blew way too early, Los Boliches' coach then got embroiled in a fight with a home fan, and there'd followed a mass confrontation involving fans and players. When Juanito (of whom I'd also seen photographs of his warmly posing with fans and, too, sitting inside Elola as a supporter himself) actually turned out for Los Boliches against Fuengirola at Elola in May 1991, and helped the visitors to a 2-1 win too, a few eyebrows had been raised; as far as I could make out, it'd been some favour involving his father.

This didn't seem to have been the happiest of marriages.

○ ○ ○

So: there were either ninety minutes or three and a half hours to kick-off. Thankfully it was the former, especially as there were no bars in the immediate vicinity, despite this being a built-up neighbourhood. I turned left off the Avenida de las Salinas onto Calle San Lucas, skirted clockwise all around the ground, cream-painted with orange and green banding, past a row of lilac trees, noticed how smart and modern CD Vera's bus looked, before arriving at the sole point of entry, which indeed was open, manned by one old chap in his seventies and a flat cap. Six euros later, and programmeless, I was in. Inevitably I lit up to take in the surroundings.

Just inside this corner entrance, raised a few steps, was a small open-air bar from where the entire proceedings would have been visible. Along this side of the wholly coverless ground were three rows of concrete, to the rear of which was a tarmacked basketball court that stretched towards an indoor games hall. Behind all of that, as on the opposite side, was a huge expanse of overlooking modern apartments. Along this side too was the odd plonked park bench. I sat on one to gaze around further. Across the low-railed, astroturfed pitch was the only stand, orange and green, half a dozen rows also of concrete, whose capacity at a guess – like Elola's – was around six hundred. It wasn't easy to guess what the entire capacity was supposed to be, because you could walk all around the pitch and station yourself at any point along the wide walkway, though you'd need to contend with trees away to the left.

Both teams were already into their long warming-up, unreached by the water sprinklers. I noticed that the Vera players, under the stern eye of their shaven-headed and hardy-looking fitness coach, were concentrating almost wholly on stretching exercises. A small farming town towards the eastern edge of Almeria province, way beyond Spaghetti Western territory, Vera lay all of two hundred miles away. I guessed that the club's budget hadn't allowed an overnight stay, so that the long coach journey, along with bleary eyes, was now being redressed. They hauled themselves up, jogged away to the far touchline, jogged all the way back and further, then proceeded to do yet more stretching by using the low rail right before me. One of them, on the left of the line, coughed up at least three green ones.

I got up, turned left, stopped at the corner bar for crisps and water, then made for the stand. Fuengirola (for that's what *Marca* still labelled them) were now doing some kicking-in. I was at Anfield once watching England play Finland and my mate got to parry the ball twice. I now kicked one and headed another, this second action provoking a second glance from the goalkeeper.

A cameraman with his young female accomplice came past and eventually I took up my own spot on the back slab overlooking the halfway line, close to a tiny raised kiosk whose scratched wooden desk was unmanned and electrical cables unconnected. From my elevated position I now had a better view of the overall milieu and saw, beyond the cosiness of the little stadium amid the apartment blocks, how pretty this was. The Sierra de Mijas rose in the background and the village itself, on this tranquil sunny Sunday, glistened in its mountain nest. I imagined how all of this might look for a night fixture – and the Estadio Santa Fe had its floodlighting – as Mijas twinkled on high.

Kick-off now near, people had trickled in. I put the attendance at around a hundred and fifty, and these included several wives, girlfriends, mates – evidently one or two of each in support of CD Vera – mothers, kids and, not an everyday sight at The Hawthorns, a one-year-old in a pram immediately to my right who thankfully slept virtually throughout. And to be honest I couldn't help but notice how delicious one or two of those wives or girlfriends looked, though I couldn't imagine that they'd ever end up using a World Cup tournament as a tabloid-recorded shopping expedition.

My old mucker Reg, I felt sure, would've appreciated all of this; but there was something missing. There were no *hinchas*, no chanting, no colours. Maybe, when Fuengirola and Los Boliches united, the passion passed away. There were folk here in support, yes, but nothing too impassioned, no frisson, very little jumping up. There was one teenaged lad, a couple of mates alongside him, with a drum, but it seemed whenever he banged on it now and again that it wasn't in any exhortation but merely because he had a noisy toy.

○ ○ ○

Spain's *Tercera Division* is divided into eighteen groups. Those that tortuously graduate from it attain *Segunda Division B* level, Spain's third, where, amid its own regionalised groupings, could be found today the likes of Rayo Vallecano, Granada and Sabadell, all with time in the top division under their belts, the former quite recently. Dotted amid this *Tercera* today, meanwhile, along with Union Deportiva Fuengirola Los Boliches (I'll call them Fuengirola for expediency's sake), were – quite amazingly, and in a prime case of financial meltdown – Real Oviedo, and none other than Barcelona's B-team for whom the likes of Xavi, Iniesta, Fabregas and Messi all once turned out, and now coached by Pep Guardiola himself. In Fuengirola's own group were Almeria B and Malaga B. Prior to kick-off, Fuengirola stood seventeenth with four wins from fourteen matches and Vera were four places above them with five more points. Whilst Vera had scored twenty-five goals so far, Fuengirola had managed a paltry ten. Enough facts and figures. I was in T-shirt and shorts, not an anorak.

Well, it took Fuengirola only two minutes to find the net now, an unmarked header by their muscular centre-forward from a free-kick away on the right. Girlfriends applauded, others stood in demi-acclaim. Now I noticed Fuengirola's coach, portly of build and in his fifties, not at all like Vera's fitness coach who was still engaged in, perhaps fixated by, more rigours down by a corner flag. Fuengirola's coaching staff, prior to the fusion, had seen not only Antonio Tapia but also, back in the 1980s, none other than Enrique Mateos, another with a lofty connection. Madrid-born, he'd been a team-mate of Kopa, di Stefano and Gento in two European Cup triumphs. This current coach reminded me facially of some old Hollywood star, perhaps Eli Wallach, but sartorially, in his windcheater (soon removed), shirt and trousers, bless him, he looked like some old advert for C&A. Soon, too, he was required to put his point of view to the linesman, who looked no older than seventeen to my eye, but whose own eye was mostly spot-on throughout.

Which is more than could be said of the referee. The old cliché is that it's a hard job. I'm not best pleased by people in their chosen jobs for whom that cliché is an excuse. I want good referees (and of course, unlike Guruceta, honest ones) who do their jobs reliably well. They're not brain surgeons or wartime code-crackers, they're football referees and they've got four other eyes to assist them. All too many of them, very sadly, are, well.... Don't talk to me about Rob Styles.

'*Mamon*!!' (Wanker) soon came the cry to my left from a stout chap in his forties, as was his target of abuse. You could hear any voice coming from the pitch (the best kind of artificial pitch, spongy when I'd felt it), and the corollary is obvious. The referee seemed to become more flustered by the minute. A minute before he'd been due to blow for half-time, just after a Fuengirola long-shot had soared even above the errants' netting to land upon someone's balcony on lilac avenue, he contracted a nosebleed that required quite lengthy attention. I doubted he'd wanted all eyes to be on him – he was just crap, not a Graham Poll – and indeed they weren't. A grandmother checked on the pram, a girlfriend dragged out a face mirror, the chief assailant felt for his fags, and a bloke in front of me unfurled *Marca*. Meanwhile away to my right amongst the trees a mongrel dog, as it would, unable right now to either mount or chew, cocked its leg.

The first half had shown up a thing or three. For one – hardly surprisingly, because after all team-mates are team-mates beyond the white line – you wouldn't have suspected that history: the home team did look well bonded. And whilst Vera had forced the play more, Fuengirola's lead was valid. And there were no fools here. Even though football's fundamentally a simple game, which doubtless helps account for its global popularity, it's not always so easy to evaluate. Would Matthews flourish today? Would Fuengirola give Scott's Leyton Orient of today a game? I looked at individuals now and thought I'd apply the tried and trusted formula of Ajax: TIPS (technique, intelligence, personality, speed)

– for the last two read character and pace in English parlance. Pace? Not much. Character? In abundance. Intelligence? Not the brightest of shows. Technique? I was seeing prevalent things here, reliably first-time ball control, easy use of either foot, deft little overhead flicks here and there to evade immediate opponents, that I doubted Reg would see at Stafford Rangers. Probably it was due to these players' upbringing, as opposed to being screamed at by fathers when aged twelve to get stuck in. Would this Fuengirola team itself hold its own in the Conference? I guessed it'd be OK one level below that. But, though a million miles away from the Sanchez Pizjuan, this wasn't a bad standard.

The second half, those kids kicking-in having duly made way, would be quite eventful. Fuengirola had made a double substitution just after the hour that included their youthful looking left-winger's being replaced by a youthful looking roving forward (those two, though, the only youthful looking players for either team), but ten minutes later they were down to ten men. A borderline offside decision that aborted a promising counter-attack had provoked protests, the number eight then incurring a yellow card from the forever agitated *arbitro*. That'd seemed to be the end of it, but the number eight must have audibly made a further comment as he stomped away, whereupon the referee – to be fair, his only cards of the game – trawled his pockets to fish out a trembling red. The player passed quite close as he stormed towards the tunnel, letting his bench know what he thought, half-turning again to thumb his scorn, his face like thunder, his weekly fix knocked on the head. Vera immediately brought on two subs of their own, both forwards, straining for at least parity in a match where both sets of back defenders were forever holding firm (not without rustic clearances) in a contest that was forever more urgent than thoughtful. And Fuengirola then sacrificed their man-mountain centre-forward in a last substitution of their own, a shoring-up decision.

Now I saw just how together, how determined, the home side was, especially after Vera brought on yet another forward for the closing minutes, around the same time that Fuengirola were reduced to nine men in a moment that encapsulated the referee's incompetence. It'd been a match played in excellent spirit but with five minutes to go came a surprisingly sly foul, too calculated to blame on sheer frustration. A Fuengirola midfielder, a combative sort in his mid-twenties and a prime protector of his back four, crumpled in front of me, facing the touchline, raked from behind in seeking a pass. The crumpling involved an angle of collapse that seemed to do a knee added damage. I heard a genuine squeal. The home bench knew what'd taken place and, led by Eli Wallach, leapt up. In fact just about everyone knew what'd happened and around me was genuine anger. The referee saw no foul and, without even waving, let play go on. Four or five aides attended to the stricken one for five minutes or so as Fuengirola's nine strove to save their lead. The stricken one then re-entered the fray to do his utmost in stoppage time. It was valiant stuff, good honest toil in which Reg would have revelled. They held on to win what'd been a wholesome contest.

After the final whistle, whooping celebration seeped from the home dressing-room beneath me as Vera's players were subjected to a warming-down out on the pitch, and Fuengirola's coach gave a filmed interview down on the touchline. Twenty minutes or so later I'd see him again when he stepped up to the bar in the corner. That sole entrance was also the sole point of exit for everyone, including the players of both teams who dawdled across the pitch, kit bags over shoulders, mobiles to ears, the odd one also calling in for more refreshment and banter among friends. It wasn't so very long ago that Fuengirola's predecessors had played league matches at La Rosaleda or against Recreativo de Huelva, and now I saw a couple of these players share a motorbike home, just like some of us used to in the Long Eaton Sunday League.

The most accomplished player on view had been Fuengirola's strolling number ten, tall in his early thirties, very comfortable on the ball under challenge, some cute passes from central midfield. But I don't know his name because Fuengirola's red shirts didn't carry any, and nor did Vera's. I saw not a soul peering from any apartment balcony. Whereas I'd seen photographs of old Elola's looking full and vibrant, not many folk seemed to care about Union Deportiva Fuengirola Los Boliches now. Having studied Paco Martin's book, I found this rather sad. After all, too, they were at a fourth level, unlike Long Eaton United or even Stafford Rangers. But I was glad I'd made the effort, anyway, to come across this different corner. I'm all for honesty and earthiness.

Juanito tragically died in April 1992, killed in a road accident, but he remains *inolvidable* not just in Madrid or Fuengirola. As a player he was hot of talent, fast of foot, and somewhat temperamental with it: everything there to be a fans' darling. I felt sure that this afternoon I'd seen no hopefuls for whom his roots might provide a real stepping-stone. But every little kid around here – and there are many whose dads have kitted them out with Real Madrid shirts – has a light that sparkles.

4

A NIGHTMARE REALITY

Tuesday 4th December

More than forty years ago now, someone daubed a question upon a wall somewhere in Liverpool: 'What Would You Do If Jesus Came Back?' Somebody else then scrawled underneath: 'Move St John To Inside-Right.'

If ever someone today in Galicia's capital city were to ask upon some wall, 'What Would You Do If St James Came Back To Life?', somebody else might just be tempted then to scrawl: 'Put Him In Charge Of Compostela.'

O O O

"Is mystic," said my friend Antonio when I told him we were going up to Galicia for a few days ('we' being myself and my 'significant other' with whom I'd been by now since May – so much for my original hopeful notion of a different kind of exploration: but we Albion supporters are a loyal breed). The trip was a good fit. Angie, born on the same day and thus somewhat conveniently named after Anglo who won The Grand National in 1966, had managed to get some time off work and fancied seeing Santiago de Compostela, for it was a picturesque and historic city; and, without being too religious herself, she was indeed a left-footer (aside from being an Evertonian). Myself, it suited entirely my desire to explore this mini-continent and it enabled me also to investigate something that particularly had caught my curiosity: how, as a fan, do you get your head around such a spectacular demise as was Compostela's?

Spain might be synonymous for all too many with sun, but for Galicia in comparison with Andalucia one could almost substitute Ireland, and a wet one at that. Lashed by the Atlantic in Spain's north-west corner, the region suffers on average over three hundred rainy days per year, making for a verdant landscape heavily wooded with oak and pine. While cows are plentiful on the scattered farmsteads, Galicia's home for a few hundred wolves too. Remote and rustic, damp and misty, wolves roaming the forests, shipwrecks galore on its *Costa da Morte* (Coast of Death): little wonder that Galicia has spouted myths and legends, even tales of witchcraft, its folk looked upon as less religious than superstitious. I'd known what Antonio meant.

Aside from werewolves and spirits heralding death, though, the biggest legend by far is centred upon the city of Santiago (Spanish for St James). Anyone sceptical about The Bible itself would most definitely give this one short shrift. The first cousin of Jesus and brother of St John, St James the Apostle had been beheaded by Herod in Jerusalem, but a couple of his mates had carted his corpse to Jaffa where a boat appeared and, though sailless and oarless, proceeded to carry them to within a few miles of Santiago. Quite why this area should have been a preferred destination, who knows, but anyone truly believing that the voyage had taken only seven days must, well, believe in miracles. Anyway, all of three-quarters of a millennium later, some hermit was drawn to a hillside by a host of stars and bones were discovered. These were said to be St James' and the hill then became called Compostela (from the Latin *campus stellae*: field of stars). The bones now lie in a crypt inside Santiago de Compostela's truly awesome cathedral, and for centuries pilgrims famously have been trekking to this spot in both homage and the hope of forgiveness. Could St James come back to life? According to one Asturian king he already did, in the year 844, fighting next to him on horseback in battle against the Moors. Inside the cathedral today were numerous confession booths manned by patiently waiting priests. No-one, certainly not my Scouse friend, took up the invitation while we were there. And I doubt that anyone afterwards sat down and said: 'Come on, father, let's be honest now. It was only ever propaganda for getting rid of all those Muslims, wasn't it?'

The list of teams that fell alarmingly down football's rankings or off the radar screen altogether is a long one. Not just clubs, but national sides too, for whatever reasons. Pele once succinctly put his finger upon the fall from grace of one Central European heavyweight by saying, 'Hungary has fallen out of love with football.' Scotland allowed itself to sink so deep that at one point it struggled to avert defeat by the Faroe Islands. Subsequently the Scots addressed their years of negligence and have now got their act back together. So too have Fiorentina, a club that actually died in 2002 but since then has stormed its way back from Italy's fourth division to reclaim its place among the elite, due to a determined city council, more so to the vagaries of the football authorities, and especially so to a wealthy new owner. But whatever happened to Dynamo Berlin? And, quite frankly, who cares? That team and its inevitable trophies were brought about entirely by the Stasi and inescapably fell by the wayside when Gorbachev realised that the Iron Curtain was shelf-expired; bizarrely, what was left of that abomination of a club then became a rallying point for neo-Nazis. Dynamo Dresden, Magdeburg, Carl Zeiss Jena? Dresden had been one of the first German cities to take this new sport of football to its heart, and the latter two clubs had reached European finals, Magdeburg even defeating AC Milan in one, but it was the new political order that largely did for them all. You can put Dukla Prague in that bracket, too, maybe even in Dynamo Berlin's.

I may be talking, as Barry might well say, bollocks, but I reckon that most clubs with a large and loyal fan-base will almost inevitably bounce back from their dire straits: one day, anyway. OK, CD Malaga provided an exception to prove the rule. But I've no doubt that Leeds United and Nottingham Forest will haul themselves back upward, just like Manchester City (quickly) and Albion (very slowly) have done in recent years. Clubs such as Villa and Wolves were never going to put up with a third or fourth level as their station. I've no doubt either that Real Oviedo will claw away here.

Reims? Enough of the long list. I'd come to Galicia now to look into Compostela, never any heavyweight, far from it, but a team that in March 1998 had lost only 1-2 to goals by Seedorf and Mijatovic in the Bernabeu before 75,000, had seven weeks later slaughtered Deportivo de La Coruna 6-2 in their own backyard, but in December 2007 languished all of four levels beneath those once heady days in *La Liga*. And if Compostela were ever to claw their way back upward, they'd have to do so without any large fan-base. Their stadium held only 14,000 and Galicia's own heavyweights were Depor and Celta de Vigo.

I'd read a bit about Compostela's dramatic sinking, but now I wanted to see just how many cared and, if they did, how they stomached their misery.

○ ○ ○

We'd clambered into a taxi upon landing and I'd immediately launched myself. There are basically two ways of learning Spanish – school or gleaning – and I preferred the latter. Angie had been here for a couple of years and gone about her own gleaning process by trying to learn grammar while she was at it. I'd decided to firstly just pick up as many words as possible and then think about verb tenses and proper sentence-forming later. I'd managed already countless stilted conversations where football was concerned, football's being in as many Spaniards' heads as it is Englishmen's and meanings thus somehow conveyed. But seeing as how Angie was with me too, she could help, I told myself.

The driver looked to be in his late thirties, stocky, dark-haired and moustached, and I'd asked him if he was a Compostela fan. He'd glanced at me but then I'd put his silence down to the manoeuvrings of airport extrication. But when the silence continued, I flashingly remembered now a couple of things of which I'd also read. You can't tar everyone with one big brush. Not all Black Country folk are salt-of-the-earth, not all Brummies are mardy, and not all Scousers are thieves. But Galicians, evidently, liked to indulge in *retranca*, a kind of mischievous reticence. An old saying throughout the rest of Spain was that, if you came across a Galician in a lift, you wouldn't know whether he were going up or down. And: Galicians, like the Basques and Catalans, had their own language (*gallego*). Not only that, but I'd read that all of eighty-five per cent of Galicians spoke it, too. Oh dear.

- "Ask him if he likes Compostela and if Caneda's still the president," I put, hopefully, to Ange.

Bless her. *Retranca* was absent now. Monologue astonishingly took over centre-stage. I managed to pick out a few key words myself, but when the albeit smiling broadside was finally over I sought a summary.

- "He says it's just a small team and maybe now for ever, there isn't any money. He says the president's more interested in being in Madrid, Barcelona. He says he only thinks small for the team. He says it's gone to rack and ruin. Do you really need me to say what he called Caneda if that was his name?"

I gave Ange some professional look.

- "He said he's a cunt."

Another thing I'd read about this neck of the woods was that its women, used to absent seafaring husbands and hardship, were pragmatic and thick-skinned. I excused the driver.

- "So is this chap a fan, or what?"
- "Ask him yourself."
So I did, and got an answer this time.
His team was Depor.

O O O

Deportivo themselves were struggling today in what were difficult times as a whole for Galician football. The 2000 champions currently occupied a relegation berth after fourteen matches, while Celta de Vigo, Champions League combatants four seasons ago, weren't finding life easy now in the second division. Racing Ferrol, true, had gained promotion the previous season to the second division, but currently lay seventeenth, while Pontevedra, a mid-table team in the top division over the late sixties, were stuck in group one of the *Segunda Division B*, where could also be found CD Lugo and CD Ourense, neither of which had ever tasted life among the elite. SD Compostela certainly had done, though, and theirs is indeed a sorry tale.

Having perennially plied their trade in the lower leagues, things improved dramatically around the turn of the nineties and indeed with the arrival of Jose Maria Caneda as the man in charge. Successive promotions in 1990 from the *Tercera Division* and in 1991 from the *Segunda Division B* had been followed by three seasons in the second tier. Just as in their later descent, arrival in the top flight had been via play-offs, Rayo Vallecano sent packing. The first season was a struggle, fifth from bottom, although eventual champions Real Madrid had been held to two 1-1 draws and among their eleven victories were a double over Celta. But over the next two seasons Compostela had finished tenth (at one point during the 1995-6 season rising to as high as second) and eleventh, the likes of Barcelona, Deportivo, Zaragoza, Bilbao, Atletico Madrid and Sevilla all being seen off in Santiago.

1998 brought heartbreak, though, and acrimony too. They

managed, while playing what was generally acknowledged to be an eye-pleasing brand of football, forty-four points: only one fewer than Racing de Santander who finished fourteenth. In those resultant play-offs, they lost out to Villarreal only on away goals, just a fortnight after their blazing victory in La Coruna. Club officials would voice their disgust at champions Barcelona for having put out a weakened side on the last day of the season, when Salamanca went to the Camp Nou and won 4-1. Had Salamanca lost, or even drawn, Compostela would have survived instead.

The bitter pill would, quickly and amazingly, assume properties that were almost cyanide. An ever deteriorating financial position was exacerbated by further relegation to the *Segunda Division B* in 2001, and whilst promotion back was immediate, so then was a relegation repeat. It was that 2002-3 season which underlined the now critical situation the club was in. In January the players, who'd even worn T-shirts in one game calling for Caneda's resignation, threatened to strike over five months' non-payment of wages, refusing to travel for a match at Cordoba. That strike was averted but, come the end of a season in which the team dutifully clambered up the table to finish ninth, SD Compostela were demoted because of their financial irregularities, the players still unpaid and Caneda unwilling to make guarantees to comply with league regulations. The following season was a similar story, but this time the players did strike, refusing to play an away fixture at UB Conquense. The resultant three-point deduction became merely statistical as the club achieved now the awful feat of being demoted two levels in the same year: to the *Tercera Division* through their league position, but straightaway consigned to the fifth level that was the Galician regional leagues, due once again to failure to meet debts and satisfy the authorities. Thus, just six years after rubbing shoulders with Barca, Real and the rest, Sociedad Deportiva Compostela found themselves beginning the 2004-5 season in the *Preferente Autonomica de Galicia, Grupo Norte*. There would follow a highly complicated situation involving tales of bankruptcy, liquidation, deferrals, transferral of rights, mergers, refounding and restructuring. There was evidently still such a state of flux when I arrived in the city, and there were at least three teams there too. One of them, Ciudad de Santiago, sat atop the *Tercera Division*'s group one, while two more were playing in that *Preferente Autonomica Norte*: Santiago de Compostela, and, at whatever the stage of their flux, SD Compostela themselves. And the erstwhile *Primera* team sat atop their pile, too. But Caneda hadn't gone away.

○ ○ ○

Santiago's an enchanting little city, all mellow granite with winding old narrow streets, arcades and squares, its pedestrianisation giving it an unhurried air, the countryside a stroll away. Galicia itself had spouted mass emigration over the years, another parallel with its Celtic kinsfolk the Irish, due also in part to famine and poverty – the largest 'Galician' city is said to be Buenos Aires, while Fidel Castro's father came from these parts (as did Franco!) – but Santiago had seen its own population almost quadruple over the course of the twentieth century. Still, it stood only at ninety-odd thousand today; and bar crawlers among them were in paradise, the abundance of drinking-holes on the Ruas do Franco and da Raina in particular being phenomenal. Though busy on this Monday night, they were civilised too, as my enquiries continued.

OK, not everyone's given to talking freely and at length about the hard times their football team's fallen upon, and I didn't expect anyone to be anywhere near as voluble as that taxi driver. Cabbies are usually willing to chinwag anyway, especially if they've been idle for a while, and that chinwagging's done in seated comfort. I doubt many standstills could be achieved on

Nottingham's pavements by someone canvassing opinion on Forest's current predicament, while in its pubs, if you could be heard above the din in any case, and then if you'd been deemed not to be some shirt-lifter, you'd likely receive just the most succinct of appraisals, probably three words at most, the middle one being an adjective beginning with 'f' and the last one a noun beginning with 's'. And not everyone's a football fan anyway.

I thought a useful indicator – and an opening – might be found somewhere over the bar staff's shoulders. Countless bars on the Costa del Sol have football scarves stuck on their walls and, whilst many might be English holidaymakers' deposits, there are many others showing allegiance to Real Madrid, Malaga or Spanish hometown clubs left behind. Ange couldn't quite get to grips with my reason tonight, wondering if I were some sort of trainspotter. "I could take you to a place in Marbella when we get back where they've got loads of different scarves." Yes, dear.

We must have drank in eight or nine bars tonight and I must have put my head inside the door of as many more. Not one Compostela scarf or pennant. The two sports shops we passed displayed the shirts of Depor, Celta, Real and Barca: not Compostela's.

I never expected, obviously, to find myself in any gloom-laden atmosphere, but I'd thought there'd be some evidence of caring for a football club that, after all, had given this city a place in the *Primera* only ten years before. When Albion sank into the old Third Division we just, after the initial tears, got on with it, drinking the beer in new places: whilst forever yearning deep inside. But pennants never came down, the latest club calendar would appear above the till, and a popular fanzine would forever prick too. In the absence here of any evidence to the contrary, I was easily and quite sadly forming an opinion that hardly anybody seemed to be bothered. This wasn't *retranca*, and if any misery had been stomached it was now lying long forgotten beneath food and alcohol.

Luis had been willing to indulge me for more than just a few moments, though. We'd eventually found somewhere to sit inside O Beiro and plonked ourselves down at a table opposite a cheery smart chap in his early forties and his smiley friend whom he also introduced to us as Rosalia. Luis conveniently, being in the hotel trade, had some grasp of English, which led to my fearing that my own friend was by now feeling ever more redundant.

– "I am not really big football fan but I can tell you something about the Compos. No, I don't go now. Maybe before if I had the chance but I liked only the big games. I think there are most people a bit like me. It is very sad what happen but today the San Lazaro is empty. I think not too many feel a need. You know, maybe, Oviedo?" I nodded. "This is no Oviedo, my friend!"

– "But there must be people here who are true fans and will not rest?" Luis' grasp missed that one. "There must be people here who want again the good times?"

– "Understand that the Compos were only all the time a little team. What happen before was miracle. Now the Compos are back. Yes, there are fans but not many. And there is no Abramovich in Santiago de Compostela!"

Luis chuckled, which led to Rosalia and Angela turning toward the pair of us, their own awkward conversation provided with an escape.

– "No-one will put money in?"

– "Who will put money in?"

– "What is Caneda doing?"

Luis pursed his lips and shook his head, mirth and disgust equally silent.

– "Caneda sits."

– "Doing nothing, or waiting?"

This question was indeed understood. Luis, now getting up, said: "Caneda has bought the rights of the old club. He sits there hoping he can then maybe make money."

As they left us, Luis ventured: "And you? Liverpool?"

Not supporting a club whose manager was Benitez or whose squad included Reina, Xabi Alonso or Torres, but one whose level didn't especially engage now residents of Galicia or anywhere else in Spain, I merely pursed my lips (as did Angela) in bidding farewell.

But Luis had told me much and, as that night wore on, his slant on things would hold. He was almost some spokesman for anyone else remotely interested in football. Basically, any replies I got would just underscore a perception that there was no real football history here, no hotbed, that some once-upon-a-time dreamland had been allowed to regress into normality, and that other things in life pressed a whole lot more. This, simply, wasn't a football town.

○ ○ ○

It hadn't rained yet and nor would it over Tuesday, which in fact was sunny. At just after two in the afternoon I went alone to SD Compostela's stadium. This now felt like a visit only of mild curiosity. The ten-minute ride to the eastern outskirts skated along a tree-lined boulevard, past the odd showroom and restaurant, then past roadsigns indicating A Coruna, Oviedo and the airport. This cabbie, slim and bespectacled with receding grey hair, looked benignly to be in his sixties. I expected nothing more than politeness, which was what I got. He said he liked Compostela but didn't go to the games. Actually, he said only two words, "*si*" to my first question and "*no*" to my last, and I wasn't convinced that he'd really understood either of them.

The stadium had been opened in June 1993 amid spacious surroundings, nudging against an expanse of rolling green fields that yielded to wooded hills. There was a huge amount of parking space all around it, but then building work had begun upon the club's initial ascent into the second division in 1991. A multi-use arena incorporating an athletics track, the main frontage stated merely 'Estadio Municipal San Lazaro': this was a council property with no displaying of SD Compostela's name. In fact the club shared this place with not only the Ciudad de Santiago outfit but also several other sporting pursuits that held offices here, including upstairs in particular one large nest of workplaces whose corridors I wandered unchallenged by any official. Back outside, a panel directed me round to door 15, the office of 'S.A.D. Compostela': those initials, while perhaps otherwise appropriate in English, standing for *Sociedad Anonima Deportiva* (limited company). Door 15 was locked up. Back at door 1 – 'S.D. Compostela Oficinas' – a tiny mailbox was visibly empty by another locked door.

I was the sole person walking around the perimeter and I found an opening that led towards the pitch. My only company inside the arena was a parked car whose open door revealed a stretched out leg, its owner asleep across the back seat. Ten minutes later this young chap, a maintenance worker, would amble over to me and I'd explain that I just wanted to have a gaze around. Other than its four distinctive floodlight towers, looking for all the world like cranes, this was no characterful place, a covered single-tiered bowl of reddish seats. The pitch – real grass – looked immaculate though, and now I found myself visualising scenes that belonged to a faded age which would most probably never have a second coming.

Compostela's shirt, halved in the Galician colours of sky blue and white and crested with the red 'Moorslayer' cross of St James, had never been worn by any household names. But among those who'd put in their shifts here had been a couple who'd participated in that lovely tournament of Euro 96: the Bulgarian centre-forward Lubo Penev, also of Valencia and Atletico Madrid, who admirably fought off testicular cancer, and Peter Hoekstra, a Dutch winger also of PSV and Ajax whom Stoke City fans would recall warmly. On the coach's bench, meanwhile, had once sat Andoni Goikoetxea, the infamous 'Butcher of Bilbao' who'd earlier left Diego Maradona and Bernd Schuster in seriously injured heaps.

But the most singular memory belonging to the San Lazaro dated from the Saturday night of 12th October 1996: a goal that Ronaldo has called his best ever. I've my own reason for recalling that genuinely fantastic goal. Bobby Robson is my all-time football hero, the root of that status being in my first ever viewing of Albion back in October 1959 at Hillsborough when, though we were two goals to the bad and reduced to nine men, Robson had indelibly ploughed ever onward through the mud till the last whistle, all pumping heart and fists-clenched refusal. Whilst I've always known that my bond with Albion was unbreakable come what may, I've always remembered Bobby Robson's, against all odds, never giving up. The man's sheer gusto for football, and his decency too, had delivered upon him wholly deserved rewards, and back in October 1996 here he'd been as the coach of no less than Barcelona. Ronaldo ran with the ball from just inside his own half, riding challenges and attempted hacks, must have jinked his way through at least half a dozen snapping opponents, before lashing the ball home. Robson had held his head as though the wonder of it all had caused it to ache, then turned to the full gathering and just stood there, asking silently: Did You Ever?

On Sunday 2nd December 2007, for a top-of-the-table game, just seven hundred had come here to see Compostela beat Somozas 1-0. *El Correo Gallego* had provided, amid its match report, a photo showing a small cluster of fans. They mostly looked – and at least half of them were female – to be in their forties or even older. They were doubtless loyal and not for giving up. I'd felt more empathy with that tiny cluster than with anything else in Santiago.

○ ○ ○

I still wanted to look at as much of this place as I could before leaving. The outside walls looked to have had much graffiti nullified but one daubing around the back remained intact:

'*Caneda - Cacique*'. *Cacique* is a brand of rum, and subsequent accompanying daubings had flippantly added '*Ron*' and '*Con Coca-Cola!*' But *cacique* is also the Spanish word for tyrant. Later tonight someone else would give me his thoughts on Jose Maria. Also around the back I noticed a couple of used condoms amid debris and some sadly disrepaired brickwork. Perhaps that said it all. The taxi driver back to the centre wasn't a football fan. He wouldn't have been interested in the fact that Compostela now aspired to Fuengirola's league.

We never introduced ourselves and I haven't a clue which busy bar it was, although its small TV was showing the Champions League game between AC Milan and Celtic. On his own, and just a bit tipsy, he'd overheard me mention Caneda to a barman who either couldn't understand me or was disinterested and, propped next to me, proceeded to enlighten me in fair English that, although Caneda, yes, had helped provide those golden days, the "directive" afterwards was "terrible". At one point, so he said, Compostela had been the only club in the top division that hadn't secured a television contract. Then Caneda had indeed threatened not to pay the players if they didn't perform to his liking. Echoing what the taxi driver from the airport had said, he'd let the club slide, wouldn't put his hand in his pocket, but still looked after number one all right. But it wasn't only the president. The town just wasn't geared up for football, there were no businessmen interested in trying or able to step in, not enough people were interested in going to the matches anyway, and many of those who'd gone previously never "felt the joy or the pain". My bar-leaning lonely and garrulous friend, who also smelled just a bit of garlic, said he felt very sorry for the few real fans. Was he one himself? No, he was just a fan of football in general, enjoyed watching the Premiership on the telly, and actually liked Manchester City because he'd spent some time in those parts and felt for their fans too "because of the shadow". At this point I actually felt myself quite warming to the bloke. I wanted to ask him what had brought him back to Galicia, but suddenly I felt a dig in my ribs.

Continuing our night stroll around the old town, a couple of things struck me: despite a scarcity of bins there was virtually no litter, and the very few patrolling policemen – who'd left unmolested at midnight a bloke happily strumming his guitar in the Praza do Toural – wore uniforms that looked curiously quite English. Again, though, no pennants or any other adornments.

Our digs, the Hostal Suso, nestled into the quaint Rua do Vilar and opposite, strangely unnoticed till now, stood the Cafe-Bar A Liga. Finally, a drinking place that connected with football. But it was empty and the two barmen were closing up, though they allowed me inside to take a look. All over the ceiling were scarves: those of various European clubs, especially Italian and English, and of numerous Spanish clubs, including even Numancia. I asked the inevitable question, which produced a shrug of the shoulders from one of them: but then a recall. He led me down the bar and pointed at a sky blue and white strip of wool hiding amongst all the other colours. At the very last – a Compostela scarf.

O O O

Worse things had happened at sea, literally so in November 2002 when *The Prestige* went adrift and its cargo of heavy fuel oil devastated the Galician coastline. A year later Manuel Rios Suarez, thirty-one years old and a father of two, had gone to the San Lazaro with his wife for a *Copa del Rey* match, had tried to stop followers of his own team, Depor, beating up a young Compostela fan outside afterwards, and received a kick to his liver from one of them so violent that it killed him.

SD Compostela are far from alone across Spain in suffering ill fate. CF Extremadura, for example, in the top flight as recently as 1999 when coached by Rafael Benitez, now find themselves at an equivalent level. Even worse, for their fans, is the story of Ciudad de Murcia. A second division club, they were bought in June 2007 by a businessman from Granada, one Carlos Marsa Valdovinos. He promptly moved the club to his own city and renamed them Granada 74, though even then they were forced to play sixty kilometres away in Motril. Real Oviedo, meanwhile, once coached by Luis Aragones and their shirt worn also by the likes of Robert Prosinecki, Viktor Onopko and the late Peter Dubovsky, not to mention the Argentinian Fernando Gamboa who infamously spat a 'great green phlegmy gozza'(Graham Taylor's words) in Nigel Clough's face at Wembley, went from UEFA Cup contestants in 1991 to the *Tercera Division* today. Indeed, due to horrendous debt and an unsympathetic mayor, the club was on the very point of extinction in 2003. But, very unlike Compostela and others, Real Oviedo is a club of some history and tradition – thirty-eight seasons in the top flight – and its fans (with a stadium big enough to still today host the national team, no less) had mobilised phenomenally in defiance. Whilst still imperilled, Real Oviedo still kicks.

I'd come to Santiago to find out how the Compostela fans dealt with their own nightmare reality. I'd anticipated maybe some typically Galician version of some everyday story of country folk, people used to adversity but who stoically find ways of dealing with their lot. Either that or they'd perhaps found solace in snorting, Galicia's coast being a major European point of entry for cocaine. But I didn't even find any Compostela fans to give my best to. Of course there were at least seven hundred of them somewhere; but even in those very much brighter days of the previous decade, the San Lazaro had all too often been less than two-thirds full, a prime example being a Wednesday night back in November 1997 when only 8,000 had turned out for the visit of Real Madrid.

Caneda, the rights-owner and evidently still some main-chancer, suspiciously likes to be some big fish. Today, so I learned, he can still be heard on national radio talking about football. He'd once upon a time given television viewers much more live entertainment by physically fighting with Atletico Madrid's ineffable president Jesus Gil, publicity which did Compostela no proper favour. Main-chancer? What main chance any more? Perhaps just some not so enhanced platform upon which to keep himself noticed, while picking some opportune moment. In the meantime, seven hundred-odd diehards will populate a pool that could only ever anyway accommodate fourteen thousand, a capacity though that now looks sadly and rather absurdly beyond any call of footballing duty.

One Galician legend had it that Santiago de Compostela was where the souls of the dead came together. While unworthy souls were destined to languish and haunt the countryside, those worthy would be taken to rest across the sea by the Sun. Now, the rain was battering the Suso's windows, would continue to batter our early morning taxi, and it was still battering the airport as we took off from a place that scarcely had a football soul.

- "Is necessary, the rain," had said the driver.

I felt fortunate to be going back to the sunshine, but more so not to be one of those seven hundred.

5

SCENES AND SCREENS
Friday 4th January

A few years ago while touring South America I'd found myself on a rickety old bus waiting to leave Copacabana, a small Bolivian town on the shores of Lake Titicaca. As I gazed out of the window an old man came shuffling across the flattened dirt that passed for the station's parking area, dodging the puddles, and proceeded in full view of everyone to pull down his stringed-together trousers, crouch down, excrete some brown cascade, then shuffle onward without wiping his backside. I'd thought to myself at the time: this isn't England. Whilst I hadn't seen anything quite like that during my first nine months in Spain, I'd certainly seen several things that hadn't either been everyday sights in England, including a young Paraguayan woman's re-enacting a deed performed next to me on that ravines-defying bus journey to La Paz by breastfeeding inside an internet cafe in Fuengirola.

One scene had especially engaged me back in July, a couple of miles along the coast one balmy Saturday night in La Cala, a small resort whose modest whitewashed dwellings emblemised a total absence of bustle, where folk simply strolled as opposed to coarsely marauding, the air easy. It was noisy now though, a night for a mass locals' party on the seafront with live music and an impromptu open-air bar. There were hundreds milling around or just squatting where they could, people of all ages including several in pushchairs, kids eating ice cream as I lolled back on a grassy bank with yet another gin and tonic. At around half-two in the morning a solitary police wagon appeared and three officers clambered out. While one was content to lean against it and light a cigarette, his two colleagues approached the bar. I'd wondered if the party were now over. What actually happened next, though, just served to enhance all the more my affection for a lifestyle that had embraced me. The two officers, in full uniform, ordered bottled beer. They then spent the next ten minutes drinking it amid the throng before leaving everyone as they'd found them.

○ ○ ○

The Costa del Sol is obviously no unique haven for the decent in an otherwise wicked world. In fact it's infamously been a bolt-hole for, let's say, dubious characters. An entertaining one, as far as I know clean too, and a team-mate on quiz nights, grew up with Ronnie Knight. Corruption in the property construction world is evidently endemic. There is organised crime, not least where narcotics are concerned. There are nightmare tales of burglary, often violent. An English holidaymaker had her handbag, containing passport and credit cards, snatched in La Cala. An acquaintance of mine tripped up a fleeing Moroccan in Fuengirola's Picasso Square which was most helpful to a screaming pack of chasing Chinese whose restaurant's takings he'd just taken. There are tales of muggings carried out at knifepoint by Moroccans, South Americans and Eastern Europeans.

Perhaps I've just lived some charmed life out here so far. But it doesn't feel charmed, not in that way. I simply haven't ever – so far – felt in the slightest uncomfortable or threatened. My relationship with my 'significant other' has naturally sunk into moments of foul discord, whereby I've stomped out at four in the morning to exorcise demons and clear my head through tramping aimlessly Fuengirola's then largely deserted backstreets.

In daylight hours this can be somewhat awkward: aside from dog owners' evidently indulging thoughtlessly their pets' needs, much so, Spaniards can tend to amble at least three abreast. But, though thus preoccupied in the dark with my thoughts and so potentially vulnerable, absolutely nothing untoward has assailed me.

I don't know the statistics and nor do I really care. Whilst President Blair's may have smacked of damned lies, others may use them as a drunkard's lamp post, more for support than illumination. I go on what I see for myself. I don't know the proportion of Spanish criminals, nor the percentage of Spanish one-parent households, nor even whether a clip round an infant's earhole is still allowed in Spain to teach effectively not only the differences between right and wrong or good and bad but also respect. But it seems to me that the dual pillars of religion and family hold sway here. When we went to Malaga just before Christmas to see its lights – somehow pastel, not in your face, and, unlike in England, not long up either – there'd been queues to enter the cathedral there on a midweek evening. Fuengirola's Plaza de la Constitucion swells with folk attending Sunday worship in its parish church. Wherever I've been in Spain, church doors have been open and at least two or three have been inside. I'm not necessarily religious myself, but I'd still like to think that folk so inclined lean towards decency. And I believe too that there's still, in Spain, much put in store by the concept of a nuclear family, whereby kids are brought up to respect and feel for not only that but also thereby society in general. Yes of course Spain has its undesirables and its football isn't hooligan-free either. But I haven't come across any gangs of drunken Spanish yobs (very different, for example, to Birmingham's Broad Street on a Friday or Saturday night), nor groups of screeching young Spanish women (they tend to be oh-so-civilised whether drinking or dining), nor indeed many instances at all of Spaniards dropping litter. On New Year's Eve, meanwhile, in the heaving Plaza de la Constitucion, I saw not a single patrolling policeman.

On such basis – and while geography obviously plays its part in some – I've witnessed scenes here that just could not happen in England today. I don't enjoy criticising my erstwhile home, my own nation. As I've already said, England is in my heart and, for goodness' sake, I've even followed its football team to places like Japan and Azerbaijan. But I truly hate the way it's gone, and I'm surely far from alone in such a sentiment, too. Whilst I've been reticent in voicing my feelings because of the risk of sounding discourteously cosy, countless holidaymakers have readily come out with the same gripes, not least one bemoaning that England's rampant disrespect with all its attendant ills is hardly surprising when you look at the culture of deceit (and the ineptitude) in the so-called corridors of power. Thus, in Fuengirola at least, there's been both a new lease of life for myself and respite for others.

For a start, I can drink wherever I like dressed however I like, and leisurely so in bars into the small hours. I can walk into a restaurant late at night in T-shirt and shorts. This is also largely the case in Malaga, Spain's fifth largest city. I am not turned away by some muscle-bound goon on the door. I've wondered what Andalucians think about their region's having become so awash with foreigners, and I think the answer lies in their pragmatism. With virtually no heavy industry, the area has historically eked out an impoverished living through fishing and agriculture. Tourism has provided jobs. Whilst taxi drivers tell me that they're pissed off by tourists' not having bothered to learn at least a few words of Spanish, they're provided with trade and thereby a livelihood. I am largely smiled upon. And Spanish beer is invariably good. I'd never had a good pint of lager anywhere in Birmingham's Mailbox despite paying three quid or more. There I go again....

In Fuengirola, even at midnight and beyond, old women will sit around together on the pavement, taking air and nattering, front doors wide open. I've walked in daylight past chairs holding only knitting or some magazine, the occupant absent but still the front door open. According to one Spanish television channel recently, the three major fears – virtually to the exclusion of any other – were the threat of terrorism (whether perpetrated by ETA or Islamists), unemployment and the economy. No mention of crime or fearsome, anti-social young arseholes. (Nor of any inevitable conflict – unvoiced in England by a silent majority but glossed over there by those, especially if seeking political kudos, who tell us it's a wonderful thing – caused by some 'multicultural society'.) Spain, it seems to me, has done fantastically well to effectively banish the ghost of Franco (the residue of anguish felt by either camp) and just get on with everything. The idea of some feral youth, high on crack and 50 Cent or some such blather, hood up and brandishing a knife, raiding some old dear's front room, is evidently not reality here. Spain's 'streets' have seen it all and today they're respected.

So I can walk along plucking oranges in danger only of treading in dog shit. I can hop on a bus without my waiting-in-line's having been ignored by usurping social boors, chip-on-shoulder Jamaicans or anyone else. I can lie on the beach at half-one in the morning amid anglers whose poles aren't kicked over for a laugh. I can go to bullfights – which indeed I have done – out of pure choice, unmollycoddled by warning, untentacled by Eurocrats, and thereby rejoice in historical tradition that, unspoken, conveys to me: this is ours, and if you don't like it yourself then you know what you can do.

○ ○ ○

Spain might be my different corner and a big country, but the world's still a small one. Who knows what secrets lurk behind its innocent little gates and doors? I'd used to work in a small railway depot, totally hidden up a dog-leg yard the other side of a set of gates, on a nondescript street in an inner-city area of Birmingham named Saltley. Anyone driving through that scruffy area wouldn't have given those gates maybe a first glance, never mind a second, but beyond them worked an inordinately polite if befuddled chap who was Joan Armatrading's brother.

Set back only a few yards off the Paseo Maritimo in Fuengirola sits Bar Gloria, run by Antonio and Petra. They've worked their socks off over many years and today have a loyal clientele of ever-returning holidaymakers (including long-stayers), expats and Spaniards. I met my argumentative Scouse friend here, but some other characters too. Bar Gloria has regularly served the following: the father of the current coach of one of the world's most famous football clubs; another inordinately polite chap who'd been a junior at that same club; the erstwhile business partner of someone who'd been chairman of West Bromwich Albion; someone who'd played for Liverpool's reserves with Phil Boersma and Roy Evans and whose daughter now arranges six-star holidays for the likes of Edwin van der Sar; and someone who played a seminal role in the rise of Dutch football hooliganism. Just an innocent bar.

I'd first got talking to 'Captain Larios' after I'd overheard his saying that everyone must've thought him some unhygienic bastard, his wearing (though ever washed) the same clothes day after day and night after night. British Airways had lost his luggage, possibly for ever. It turned out he was a Tottenham fan. "An' I used t'fight for 'em, too!" Though somewhat wizened by his perpetual alcoholic fix, other things his gravelly voice came out with made it so that we must have been of a similar age. So we delved back into the lost – for me, at least – days of glory-chasing, and a particular trophy in a particular year had then consumed the rest of the conversation. Yes, he'd been there in Rotterdam in 1974 when Feyenoord won the UEFA Cup amid mayhem. "The police were barsteds, they just took their side, but we never fakkin' ran." Captain Larios looked into his gin, tittered and looked back up to me. He looked about seventy now, this wrinkled but cheery Jew who'd helped via television screens to enthuse a whole new generation into developing their own copycat shenanigans, whereby ultimately the leader of Ajax' *F-Side* would be murdered on wasteland by the baseball bats and iron bars of Feyenoord's *Vak S*. Christ, the aged mellowness today!

The famous son's father, meanwhile, had first been pointed out to me as he'd sat on a bar stool in the Gali Gali bar-restaurant by the beach. Soberly dressed, black, flat-capped, he'd been sipping some fruit juice and I'd noticed the staff's paying him special attention as if they were all seeking the latest titbits. I'd bump into him numerous times after that, whether just to reciprocate his ever-polite "hello" as he glided slowly and seemingly carefreely along the Paseo, or to find him relaxing on Bar Gloria's terrace. I've never intruded into Herman's relaxation by probing his thoughts on football, for two reasons. He's evidently not in the very best of health nowadays – well looked after, a car ferries him regularly to Marbella's hospital for his condition to be treated – and I'd been told by Angela (with whom he occasionally likes to chat about other things) that, simply and entirely understandably, he'd become rather tired of people forever wanting to know what he had to say on the game, pumping him for information about one of his sons in particular. But I know that he'd been a player himself, in Brazil – "all the money they get now, and they used to pay us in oranges!" he'd chortled – and I know that he enjoys his regular stays on the Costa del Sol as a welcome change from the shivers of Amsterdam. I look at Hermo and try to picture him as he once was, setting out from Surinam for a bravely uncertain new life in northern Europe, and I tell myself that he must feel so, so proud today. His surname, of course, is Rijkaard.

Another very proud man right now is Lluis, because his lovely Swedish partner has just presented him with their first child, a son. Lluis is one of the many personable characters that I've met in my time here. He still plays, earns a living as a motor mechanic, and his humility never allows him to bang on about his earlier time as a junior at Barca where he'd rubbed shoulders with names that subsequently became household. A right-sided attacking midfield player himself – "like Figo!" he'd laughed – his big friend had been Albert Celades, the Andorran who went on to play for Spain and Real Madrid too, currently still playing at Zaragoza. 'Chappy' Ferrer, later of Chelsea, had been another mate. Lluis, though, retained special admiration for Pep Guardiola, and certainly not just because, like himself, he was a real Catalan. He saw again now those images of yesteryear, shook his head, blew, and pointed everywhere: "ping!....ping!....ping!...." Lluis' English is roughly akin to my Spanish but Sophia, his partner, is wonderfully fluent in both. As in Hermo's case, I hadn't wanted to pry, but Sophia had been both accommodating of myself and supportive of Lluis in describing what had happened. "Lluis would open his mouth, argue against what he thought was wrong. Some of that against him was, yes, political. In the end, his face didn't fit." But none of that had ever soured Lluis' love of the club. I'd be given ample evidence of that one Sunday night just before Christmas.

○ ○ ○

One could argue till the cows do the proverbial about the merits or otherwise of television's mass coverage of football. Among the cons might be the loss of a level playing field through the distribution of money and a loss of mystique because the global game is now so readily on tap. I try to be pragmatic in telling myself that it's nice to have such availability and if I don't want to watch then I don't have to.

There's certainly an availability over here: Dutch bars showing live *Eredivisie* games, stations such as Canal Plus showing almost everything including live *Bundesliga*, *Serie A* and *Ligue 1* games, Latino bars showing live Argentinian and Brazilian matches – and of course Spanish bars showing not only the *Primera* but also the odd second division game. I'd obviously used to lap up Sky's coverage of Spanish football back in England but I'm bound to say that it feels so much better to watch such fare with Spanish commentary in the company of Spaniards: as far as television allows (there's really nothing like being there), it feels more authentic and indeed more entertaining when it comes with locals' jabberings and exclamations. I enjoy finding little backstreet bars wherein I really do feel in Spain, and very often – especially when Real or Barca are involved – such places will be quite busy because many folk can't afford domestic access to pay-per-view football, which is the way of things here now (yes, indeed, the rich get richer in Spain too – Real Madrid's current TV deal with Mediapro, for example, wholly in contrast to those negotiated by the likes of Levante, is worth 157 million euros a year).

So, in settings of demi-authenticity, I'd also lapped up the *Copa America* back in the summer, for I came to realise then just how many South Americans now live in Fuengirola. Bars such as Cuba Libre, Tahiti and Bocaccio would have the national flags of Uruguay, Chile or Paraguay draped across their chair backs, and there'd be the instantly identifiable Andean faces of Peruvians or Bolivians glued to the early morning screens. When Claudio Pizarro headed an 85th-minute equaliser for Peru, it meant that they, instead of their desperately unfortunate opponents Bolivia, had qualified for the quarter-finals; but there were simple handshakes around me between the generous and the resigned. My most abiding memory of that tournament, though, was the sight of a teenaged Uruguayan, resplendent in the national shirt and all by himself, sat forever hunched forward on a sofa in Cuba Libre, though his soul was away in Maracaibo for the semi-final against Brazil: anxiety and entreaty etched all over him with the odd unashamed prayer thrown in. The game went to a penalty shoot-out which Uruguay threw away, though Brazil's goalkeeper Doni had been ridiculously three yards off his line when making the matchwinning save. The young kid sprang from his seat, turned round and booted it, thunderstormed his way to the door in tears, and rather worryingly spurted off on his scooter. As for the final itself, which kicked off at an hour when thoughts were already turning towards breakfast, the aftermath of physical Brazil's three-nil victory had sadly been the sights of a lone Brazilian's being chased along the beach by half a dozen Argentinians and a Brazilian family's enduring catcalls from another group; there'd been countless Argentinians thronging the bars throughout the competition and at least half of them had Messi's name on the backs of their shirts.

Tommy's Bar-Cafe, not far from the bullring and whose owner had been born in Argentina to parents who'd fled there from Nazi Germany, and of course Bar Everest, had been just two places to sample what was on offer. In early November I'd heard Cristobal from yards away up the street: 'Oieeee!!' and 'Ay-Ayy-Ayyyeee-Oieeee!!' Real were playing Olympiakos in Greece in a Champions League group game that finished goalless for all the eccentricity gushing out from behind the bar. I couldn't begin to describe the noise I heard when van Nistelrooy lobbed onto the crossbar after half an hour. Nor have I ever pointed out to Cristobal that one of his two bar signs actually says 'Bar Everets'. A moment of relief, meanwhile, had occurred earlier in the season in Bocaccio, packed for Barcelona versus Athletic Bilbao. That bar is a known haunt of Moroccan prostitutes – female ones, that is – but midway through the second half the bloke in his late sixties immediately to my left had nudged me and pointed to his crotch. Jesus. But he'd only wanted me to save his seat.

So, on the Sunday evening of 23rd December, there we all were in Bar Gloria: Angie behind the bar, myself on the TV's side of it along with an edgy Lluis, a massive Sophia, a handful of Lluis' family down from Barcelona, and several locals. Sky's commentary was turned off in favour of a frenetic Spanish radio. It was an unsurprisingly tense and bitty contest where Barca — without the injured Messi — had actually looked to be stepping up a gear as the first half stuttered on, the only goal against the run of play. But Barca never got into any stride, fluency was absent, and their cagey visitors looked increasingly comfortable. Ronaldinho — his star at the Camp Nou now troubled amid accusations of unprofessionalism and lack of caring — and Eto'o were both poor. The goal came in the thirty-sixth minute, Baptista pushing the ball to van Nistelrooy thirty yards out, van Nistelrooy dinking first-time back into Baptista's muscling run, the Brazilian lashing right-footed high past Valdes from just inside the box. Real Madrid thus went seven points ahead at the top of the table. Lluis would of course be more than consoled by the thought of little Lucas inside Sophia's tummy, but for more than just a few moments his head wasn't working like that.

Myself, I was learning more about Spanish football by picking my way through *Marca*, talking with the likes of Lluis (for example, I hadn't known till now that Carles Puyol, Barca's heart-on-sleeve captain, had actually started out as a forward), and, besides taking on board the televisual offerings, going to matches too (Malaga, when I'd visited La Rosaleda again, had looked much better against Las Palmas, more together and assured, and were pushing strongly for promotion).

I wasn't kidding myself, though.

○ ○ ○

I'd been back a few times to watch Albion since emigrating, most recently in late November for a goalless home draw with Wolves. The original idea then had been to take in also England's last Euro 2008 qualifying match against Croatia at Wembley, but after the failure in Moscow I'd decided to deaf that one out since it'd taken on the hallmark of a dead rubber. *Sin embargo* (somehow my favourite Spanish expression): however. I'd watched Russia then lose to Israel in Frank the Manc's bar and said to him: "I've got to go." So I booked up another set of flights (I've a lifelong friend, Steve Clark, with whom I'd once worked at The FA and who still, bless his heart, sees me right for England tickets). Thus it was that I flew from Malaga to Gatwick on the Wednesday, back again the next morning, then from Malaga to Birmingham two days later and back again on the Monday. Dossing around all night at a Gatwick airport awash with Croatians after they've just knocked you out of Europe was almost as painful an experience as Zoltan Gera's missed penalty against our Black Country 'neighbours'. One or two of those Spaniards in Bar Gloria consider me a touch mad whilst, I think it's fair to say, one or two others take their hats off to me, albeit chucklingly. I certainly hadn't done any chuckling myself after England's showing. Peter Crouch apart, they were truly disgusting.

But The Baggies are my team and they always will be. It sometimes feels as though I've come full circle, for as a child I'd waited for their results on *Grandstand*'s teleprinter and now, in Bar Gloria, I find myself often watching *Gillette Soccer Saturday*, hunched forward like that Uruguayan kid. For two hours I want to talk to no-one, and don't, except to Ange who'll entice me into another one but otherwise knowingly keep her distance as I watch out for the latest scoreline. And I hide the remote. Someone saw me fish it out from the bookcase after our recent televised win against Charlton but I've found somewhere else since. As a last resort there's always my underpants and I kid you not.

I'd actually found myself squirming in my seat towards the end of that Malaga-Las Palmas game, as the visitors went close to equalising prior to Malaga's sealing their fully deserved win with a second goal in stoppage time. I thought about that afterwards. It was good that Spanish football had engaged me to such a degree: I'd been seeking that something different to feel inside.

But I knew that my discomfort had been only for those marvellous *Malaka Hinchas*. Malaga weren't, and never could be, my team.

○ ○ ○

After Real's triumph at the Camp Nou, *La Liga*'s season shut down for a fortnight. With seventeen of thirty-eight matches done, Espanyol sat third, Atletico Madrid in fifth had somewhat flattered to deceive, Racing de Santander in sixth were proving to be nobody's mugs, Valencia were in chaos, while Sevilla's results were either hot or cold, seven wins but unthinkably (never mind Juande Ramos' defection) eight defeats. Deportivo were in a perilous position, next to bottom. Betis and Bilbao were again in danger too. But only four points separated Deportivo from Zaragoza in ninth. None of the three promoted sides – Almeria, Murcia and Valladolid, who'd all managed to win on the opening day of the season – were in the bottom three.

Around the corner lay the business end of the campaign. So I thought it was time now to sample the top. But, in the next match I'd go to, I'd be very interested also in the away side, for to me they were torch-bearers in (and despite) football's new age.

-6-

BINOCULARS AT THE BERNABEU

Sunday 27th January

I'd paid Madrid merely fleeting visits in the past, solely to change trains or aeroplanes within schedules that allowed nothing more. This time, though, and whilst it'd still felt that I'd be only scratching its surface, I'd have seventy-two hours in Spain's capital city. Lluis, of course, had wished me a good time – and then, of course, had given me the thumbs-down for Real Madrid. On my second glimpse of the place over thirty years previously, on my homeward journey from that Guruceta-spoilt trip to Alicante, I'd noticed people living in caves on the city's outskirts. Now – no trains other than its metro involved, but just a fifty-minute flight from Malaga – my agenda held two priorities: a particularly infamous cave, and a world-renowned football theatre.

○ ○ ○

The ball they used was the 'Improved T' football manufactured, complete with laces, by Wm Thomlinson Ltd of Dumbarton Road. Among the adverts in the one-shilling match programme, whose front cover featured a coin being ceremonially tossed by a referee wearing a blazer, was one advising to 'Never go without a Capstan – Scotland's largest-selling cigarette', while Sellyn's offered easy repayment terms of five shillings weekly over forty-two weeks for a man's suit, thus 'leaving holiday savings intact' (alternatively, you could 'choose from the latest gay cotton'

82

for a dress or jumper suit). The language of that era also manifested itself in the players' pen-pictures: penned by flowery wordsmiths, perhaps in copperplate at first. Marquitos, the right-back, had 'revealed his invaluable generalship and foresight'. Of di Stefano: 'There were those who whispered he was approaching a time when he would be compelled to give way to insurgent youth, but he once again disclosed his genius against Barcelona in the semi-final.' The right-half Vidal was a 'most thoughtful purveyor' who could 'kill the most capricious ball'; del Sol, the inside-right, 'makes the ball answer his will'; Gento, at outside-left, was a 'mesmerist'. As for the Germans, goalkeeper Loy had 'his efficiency thrown into relief in the semi-final against Rangers'; Hoefer, the left-back, was 'exceedingly difficult to circumvent....no matter how fierce and scientific assaults become'; Kress, the outside-right, was 'a gay deceiver'. Bob Kelly, the Scottish FA president, had meanwhile anticipated that 'we shall be regaled by the artistry and genius of the finalists', which 'should make this one of the most memorable matches in the history of the game'.

Well, we were; and it was, and still is.

Manchester United fans are not alone in their wonderment that three major luminaries such as Charlton, Law and Best could all line up together, and Dutchmen and Brazilians among others will point to their own dreamy assemblies. But there is something almost pulverising about an image of Alfredo di Stefano and Ferenc Puskas both hovering over the ball in their white strip at kick-off and Francisco Gento awaiting it. Even the very surnames sounded spellcasting to me, 'di Stefano' conjuring thoughts of fine art and 'Puskas' of some smoking cannon. May 18th, 1960. Burnley were champions of England, The Beatles were unheard of, and I was at primary school. While children younger than us would chirp out nursery rhymes in the playground, some of we nine-year-olds would determine to memorise the 'Reel Madrid' line-up of that night. That I've ever since been able to reel off one to eleven is less to do with my power of recital and a whole lot more to do with the imprint that awesome performance made. It was poetry and potency incarnate, at once both beautiful and violent, the quintessence of a football ideal. I'd already fallen in love with football by then but I hadn't known it could be that wonderful. It says something that, even forty-eight years later in today's unscrupulous age, that display is still revered. In my new different corner, I was always before long going to take myself to the Bernabeu, for reasons of sentimentality and the real hope I could still be charmed now.

Kick-off was 9pm on the Sunday. I landed at Barajas airport at half-one on the Friday dinnertime and had other things to attend to first.

○ ○ ○

Having been a bit worried that I might have difficulty actually getting in to see the match, I'd decided to book a ticket online prior to leaving home. This was fine, and I'd felt glad that I'd done so because most of my preferred west stand was evidently sold out already. But a difficulty would subsequently arise. The club's website had an English language version and the tickets section, having guided me through the transaction, duly told me in my own tongue that my purchase had been made successfully and provided details of my seat, the total cost and a reference number. But: the information beneath the heading 'Where can I pick up my tickets?', quite crucial after all, wasn't in English, it was solely in Spanish.

The metro from the airport deposited me at Nuevos Ministerios from where I'd intended taking line 10 southward to Tribunal, a station close to the digs I'd earmarked. But I'd noticed that Santiago Bernabeu was conveniently just one stop northward from Nuevos Ministerios on the same line, so it was ticket first and digs later. Things were about to become doubly awkward.

Having determined to wait till the day of the match itself to absorb properly the setting, and thus allowing myself now only a brief awestruck gaze, I made for the ticket office. There must have been at least five hundred people forming a queue whose head disappeared through a huge gateway with not an official in sight. Bugger that. There was a bar nearby built into the stadium and a girl there told me I could collect instead from gate so-and-so. When I arrived at gate so-and-so a man shook his head and directed me to another gate so-and-so. Having traipsed round to this other gate so-and-so, someone there also shook his head and instructed me to go a hundred yards or so around the corner to a shopping mall and look for an official Real Madrid merchandise shop, which would accommodate me. It couldn't. Inside my head now was not so much a recall of that palaver I'd had on my first visit to La Rosaleda, but a vow that over my dead body was I going to leave this place without my paid-for bloody ticket. There was another bar inside the mall. The barman pointed me towards a nearby nest of machines. The machines obviously required some card to be inserted but I hadn't a clue what card – maybe some kind of club card – and there was nobody to ask. Outside the stadium again – having done virtually an entire circuit – I happened across a window. I showed the man behind it my Realmadrid.com proof of purchase and asked him, flexing my fingers in readiness to reach through and throttle him if he couldn't. He asked for my bank visa card. When he duly handed it back, details checked, it was with my match ticket. He told me I could have done all this at any of numerous machines and pointed this out on my Realmadrid.com sheet of paper.

I still haven't told Barry from D's Bar in Fuengirola that I'm writing this book, but someone else has, and apparently his immediate reply was: "Him?! Write a book?! He can't write a bloody book, he's too bloody thick!!" Barry has also threatened to have Angela sectioned.

But how come that barman in that mall had been the only one?

So, having thus spent roughly as long at the Bernabeu as I would two days later, I made for the metro again. I'd earmarked those digs from a guidebook and had wanted to book those in advance too. I suppose I should have smelled a rat when its website said it was currently unable to take bookings online, but the website had indeed been still there and so it was surely reasonable to believe that the Hostal Barajas itself would be too, conveniently located in Malasana, an old working-class area good for experiencing the city's soul, for nightlife too, and quite close to the main sights. I trudged along Calle Augusto Figueroa, bag over shoulder now quite heavy, then backtracked having seen no sign. Now I was seeking actual street numbers. An old woman clad in black stood by number seventeen which was where the Hostal Barajas, formerly 'unusually well appointed', had ceased to exist. And dusk was setting in.

Sod's Law has it that you'll inevitably come across loads of places to stay when you're no longer seeking one but, while such need persists, finding somewhere must take on the properties of the proverbial needle. Even in Madrid. My budget was much less Real's and much more Levante's, and all I sought were clean bedsheets and my own shower, never mind how poky and scruffy the outside (and unnoticeable the sign). Having left Calle Augusto Figueroa some distance behind and still with no joy, but having wandered into a very busy quarter, I sought help in a corner bar, now brightly lit, where a man gave me some disbelieving look before quite theatrically sweeping an arm that said: take your stupid pick all along down there. The first place on Calle Hortaleza I tried was, well, unsuitable. Climbing its four flights of dim stairs, the stench of stale urine together with the graffiti and smeared snot on the decaying walls reminded me of long-ago visits to the city of Real Madrid's most famous triumph, Glasgow; that I could have put up with, but the grubby showers were shared – and there seemed something dubious about the sexagenarian owner, a man with four fluffy white little dogs. Eventually, then, I ended up in the Hostal Gaudi, which was suitable enough. Within a minute of having stepped back out, though, I saw two male couples walking hand-in-hand. I'd landed in Chueca, the gay quarter of Madrid. A few hours later I'd walk into La Sastreria, just across the street from my window, thankfully still serving at half-two in the morning, full of young couples, not a woman in sight, and pay an arm and a leg for a small beer. I'd suspected I'd been charged in excess of the going rate, but doubted the barman's name was Richard Kress.

O O O

Writers much cleverer than I have painstakingly and sleuth-like attempted to tell whether or not Real Madrid received favours (with the obvious corollary) from the Franco regime. It seems, of course, to be taken as read in Catalonia that they did, as a natural extension of that region's separatist desire being held firmly under the thumb of a Madrid-based fascist dictatorship, its Catalan language – literally, the very expression of a culture – of course banned too. In his marvellously informative book *Morbo* that deals with the rivalries driving the game in Spain based upon its regional, historical and political differences, such independence of spirit felt especially by the fans (this being one of two particular bibles I read before leaving England, Giles Tremlett's also wonderful *Ghosts Of Spain* being the other), Phil Ball tells how Santiago Bernabeu's grand vision for Real Madrid upon assuming its presidency in 1943 sat with a wider ideal of *El Caudillo* himself: acceptance, not least abroad, through glory. As Tremlett informs, two salient factors towards the eventual reassimilation of Franco's shunned corner were, firstly, an allowing of American air bases on Spanish soil as the Cold War became ever frostier, and, very pragmatically too, and comparatively trivial though it may seem (but truly groundbreaking), an official nod to bikinis, thus welcoming the mass tourism that would bestow salvation upon a dreadful economy. But nothing is more glorious than glory. When Real Madrid – and, for all their exoticism, six of those eleven were Spaniards – demolished Eintracht Frankfurt 7–3 at Hampden, Franco's Spain became associated with shining heroes based in his capital city.

A couple of Ball's revelations would arm the conspiracy theorists. If Santiago Bernabeu, decorated during the Civil War for his support of Franco's cause, had been the father of Real Madrid, then the son who came to make it all happen was Alfredo di Stefano. Back in 1953 di Stefano was set to become a Barcelona player but was snaffled by their great rivals instead, and Ball describes how a Barca negotiator claimed that Franco's men had bugged his telephone among other acts of sabotage. And then, in 1972, a referee named Antonio Camacho actually came out and said that Barcelona would never be champions as long as the current president of the National Committee of Referees, a Madrid sympathiser named Jose Plaza, sat in office. (And, as we have seen, at least one Spanish referee could be bought.)

On the other side of the conspiracy coin, it could be pointed out that Barcelona won the Spanish championship no less than eight times during the Franco years, and that it was nobody's fault but their own that they blew their chance of European Cup glory against Benfica in 1961, having eliminated Real along the way.

There is no doubt that Franco benefited from Real Madrid, the image they provided. Whether the club received a helping hand here and there in return on the field of play, who, aside from any perpetrators themselves, could say? If they were so favoured, it was a million miles away from the gerrymandering that enabled Dukla Prague to dominate in Czechoslovakia, and much further still from the ridiculous shenanigans that saw Dynamo Berlin prevail in East Germany. Franco wasn't stupid. And, saviour or tyrant, I couldn't come to Madrid, capital city of this intriguing land that was now my home, without paying his final resting place a visit.

His tomb lay thirty miles north of Madrid within a vast ornate basilica hewn out of a granite ridge of the Sierra de Guadarrama. Lording above, built of stone, stood reputedly the tallest memorial cross in the world, all of a hundred and fifty metres high. Buried nearby in *El Valle de los Caidos* (The Valley Of The Fallen) were forty thousand, both Nationalists and Republicans, and the entire monument is said to be in commemoration of the Civil War dead of both persuasions. But the monument, built to Franco's orders, took twenty thousand slave-labourers eighteen years to complete, during the course of which fourteen of them died, and those slave-labourers were all Republican prisoners. The only two marked tombs, by the high altar, are those of Jose Antonio Primo de Rivera and Francisco Franco himself, the former the Falange's founding father and Franco's mentor. Solely names appear on the tombstones, nothing more, but you don't have to look far to be told: 'Fallen for God and for Spain!' Two old women stood over Franco's stone looking wistful and crossing themselves, and one dabbed an eye. No-one could deny that Spain had been in an unholy fragmented mess when he grasped the nettle, but this whole spooky place smacked of gaudy triumphalism to me, and seemed even contrived, a bit like lion statues outside some suburban detached house, yet as if Franco really had considered himself some God's lieutenant. The Spanish Civil War, an ideological mayhem, vicious, is entirely fascinating to outsiders, but the vast majority of Spaniards have pledged to bury that past and try to forget the Franco years. As a fascinated outsider, I was glad I'd come to this Valley but wasn't sorry to leave.

○ ○ ○

- "Whereabouts did you stay?" would ask Petra after I'd got back.
- "I was in The Ritz." (Cue dropped jaw.)
Well, I was, but only for five minutes, and in between the urinal and the mistakenly fawning doorman I found it difficult

to understand how so very many people were content to sip tea upon pink sofas on such a beautifully sunny afternoon. It was Sunday now, matchday, and I was enjoying a hop-on-and-off open-topped bus tour of the city, the weather in fine contrast to that during my similar tour of Barcelona the previous March when I'd been battered by a hailstorm. I'd already sampled a couple of historical sites – *El Escorial*, the palace-monastery of Felipe II, a short bus ride from Franco's cave, and home of he who sent forth the Armada, then on Saturday night I'd sat in grand Plaza Mayor, sipping arm-and-a-leg coffee and picturing Inquisition killings – but this bus seemed the best way to scratch that surface of a few more sights, including inevitably the Prado and the Royal Palace. It also took me past Cibeles Square to whose fountain Real's fans traditionally head in celebration. Now and again, armed as I was with a postcard that showed a Madrid of the late fifties with its dinky-toy cars, I'd try to imagine how it really was all those years ago in di Stefano's heyday. But, despite a sad proliferation of graffiti, I couldn't help but be struck by the city's grandeur today. Or, in fact, by its cosmopolitan air: believe it or not, of the one hundred and ninety nations recognised by the UN, people from no less than a hundred and eighty-three of them now live in this city.

The city tour's blue route actually took in the stadium, but I wanted to emerge from that metro station again.

O O O

Not that the Bernabeu needed to, but football stadia can seem somehow to take on added spirit in the hours of darkness, as if infused by the electricity. They appear to dominate the landscape all the more; bands of faces come into focus from some shadowed mass as if to herald the approaching kick-off; even sounds and smells seem to carry more resonance; inside, depending of course on how characterful or otherwise they are to begin with, the stands can seem more evocative of past deeds; the vim of support is caught by floodlighting unwilling to let go. Home FA Cup replays on January or February nights had often felt special like that. When Alfredo and the rest had so been at it here in pursuit of the topmost pot, it could only have been....well, that I would try to imagine upon taking my seat.

The air was thick tonight as I made the pavement into the swarm, approaching the stadium's south-west corner. The Avenida Concha Espina that ran behind the south stand had been closed to traffic and so the swarm was buzzing freely. Stalls galore were set up now selling scarves, souvenirs and sustenance. A lad barely into his teens wanted two euros for a small bottle of water and an old woman was demanding, unbelievably, eight euros for a bag of sweets. I edged inside the Brio bar on this corner and back out again with a very reasonably priced beer. Now I soaked up the scene and there was no doubt I was surveying something special, not just because of its legends but also for the reason that the Bernabeu looked genuinely stately, a sumptuousness about its symmetry. Whilst they certainly look from the outside like football settings should, some grounds radiate that extra something, a ready sense of theatre. Old Wembley had it in its idiosyncratic way. So too the Bernabeu tonight in its sophisticated way.

Given its location, though, it could hardly be allowed to look anything less than elegant, never mind that it housed such an illustrious football club. Casting my eye away for a moment from the buzzing Concha Espina as anticipation mounted there in the glow, I glanced to my left: to the city's poshest boulevard and site of one of the most outrageous deals ever made, and one that convinced so many folk all the more that Real Madrid was indeed the favoured club of the Establishment even with Franco long dead.

Its star had waned over the years. Whilst still collecting domestic titles, the aura abroad in an ever-developing landscape had been invaded by the likes of Cruyff's Ajax, Beckenbauer's Bayern, Paisley's Liverpool and Berlusconi's Milan. Two UEFA Cups – a competition that Real had previously vowed never to enter on the grounds that, demeaningly, it was only for also-rans – had been won in the mid-eighties; but, after 1966, that topmost pot would elude them for all of thirty-two years. The sheen had worn away. And, by the time that Florentino Perez snatched the presidency in the summer of 2000, so had the finances: Real were all of £173 million in debt. That hadn't stopped Perez, though, from immediately splashing out a further £37 million to cutely prise Luis Figo away from Barcelona, a promise he'd made to the fans so that they'd vote him in. And Figo had been only the first, as Perez now embarked upon a policy of bringing in at huge cost a succession of world stars (attacking players, that is) – the 'galacticos' project – that he'd considered would keep the fans happy by 'giving them the best players and the greatest entertainment'. As we all know, it was a flawed policy, suspiciously driven mainly by commercial reasons, 'maximising the brand', though Perez doubtless expected those players to deliver the required pots too. To begin with they did: apart from winning *La Liga* in 2001 and 2003, Real, as they'd also succeeded in being in 1998 and 2000, were champions of Europe again in 2002. But between 2003 and 2007: zilch. In his very revealing autobiography, Steve McManaman had spoken of growing divisiveness, lesser mortals (though key defensive players such as Claude Makelele) left feeling undervalued, and the 'Disneyfication' of it all; and of scant attention paid, certainly not in the transfer market where defenders were concerned, to the needs of the team when the opposition had the ball. Ivan Helguera, one of those beleaguered defenders, had also bemoaned a dilution of spirit, while Michel Salgado had spoken in late 2003 of 'five players that have to work as a team and five that you can't oblige to do so'. I'd seen to my personal cost how disjointed and frankly uncommitted Real had so often looked in the meantime: numerous were the Sunday

Why? indeed. Spain mourns Sevilla's Antonio Puerta

A man with a vision – Real Madrid's new president
Santiago Bernabeu engages his imagination in 1943

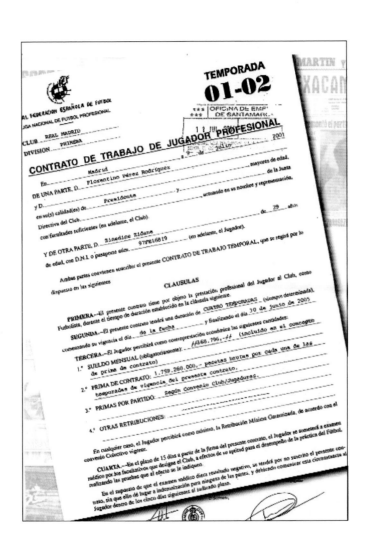

A *galactico*'s contract

The birthplace of Spanish football – Huelva's *Casa Colon*

Respect, please! Recreativo lay on thick their oldest-member status

San Mames and its tastefully grand arch

Not the best vantage point for ninety euros; nor the best result for
Barcelona at Almeria

The joy of promotion! Malaga's fans celebrate at La Rosaleda

Binoculars at the Bernabeu as Real and Villarreal compress the play

All quiet on the Avenida Concha Espina – Friday afternoon outside the
Bernabeu, not an everyday place

Ronald Koeman's last match as Valencia's coach as Athletic Club Bilbao
inflict a 5-1 drubbing inside *'La Catedral'*

Past and present –Rio Tinto's old railroad with the
Nuevo Colombino in the background

A founding father bares all by Recre's original stadium

nights I'd gone to bed cursing, my fixed-odds coupon lying just one tick short in the bin.

Back, then, to cost. How had Perez found all that money to not just finance his grandiose project but also, even having done so, help put the club firmly in the black?

That posh boulevard is the Paseo de la Castellana. Between its trees, aside from a statue of Columbus, can be seen in all their des-res splendour a museum housing works by El Greco, Rembrandt and Goya, ministerial buildings including those for the Environment and Defence, and assorted business establishments which include Madrid's once tallest skyscraper, the 43-storeyed Picasso Tower that was designed by the same architect who'd given New York its ill-fated twin towers. Further up the Castellana had once lain Real Madrid's huge training headquarters, on a designated greenfield site. In mid-2001 Perez brokered a deal with the local authorities that would see the club's facilities demolished, the site expediently reclassified to enable four huge new office towers to be built there instead (each of them higher even than the Picasso), and the club thereby receive over £300 million from the local authorities for the sale. Given that the city hall and the regional government were both on the political right – long viewed as harbouring a mutual preference for Real Madrid – foul was cried by all and sundry including, predictably, the presidents of Barcelona and Atletico Madrid and, indeed, the left side of Madrid's politicians. In a single stroke, Perez had thus both seen off Real's massive debt and armed himself with massive funding.

But it would need Fabio Capello's iron fist to bring another trophy to the Bernabeu, and only then because both Barca and Sevilla frittered away their own chances of that 2007 league title.

○ ○ ○

To say that the away side tonight provided contrast would be quite outrageous too, but only for the understatement. For those like myself, rendered defeatist by football's new way of things, they shone boldly a challenging light. At this point, I'll say two things: firstly, by Christ I want to be proved wrong about English football's future; secondly, challenge is accommodated much more so in Spain than in England. In England, who can ever surmount the 'big four' of Manchester United, Chelsea, Arsenal and Liverpool? (Even Liverpool have failed so far to actually win the Premier League, and furthermore they've never even looked like winning it up to now.) Spain? Surely that's just a matter of Real Madrid and Barcelona? But since 1992, the year of The-Not-The FA Premiership's inception, and despite too the recasting of the European Cup into a heavily-seeded process that favours and enriches still more the elite, and despite Bosman, Spain has allowed something more. Atletico Madrid have won the double. Deportivo de La Coruna have won the championship. Valencia have won it twice. Valencia have also reached two UEFA Champions League finals. Both Deportivo and Real Sociedad have genuinely had the Spanish championship in their grasp only to let it slip away at the death. Sevilla really should have won it last year, too.

And then there's tonight's visitors to the Bernabeu:Villarreal.

A comparison might be made with Wimbledon, another fairytale ascent. But their meteoric rise, from amateur ranks to top-division status and FA Cup winners, gave hope to all at a time when English football was a level playing field prior to its financial distortion.Villarreal's spectacular and rapid progress – in a town of just 48,000 left wholly unmentioned by the *Rough Guide* – has been made during a period of burgeoning elitism, thus providing a beacon of inspiration for all who might otherwise consider infiltration today to be an unrealistic proposition. In truth, they've prospered through having a benefactor – Fernando Roig, a ceramics multi-millionaire – but glasses should still be raised, as have been several eyebrows along the way.

Founded in 1923, they were still in the regional backwaters as quite recently as 1977, and even in 1991 were at the level where Fuengirola are today. Roig became president at the end of the 1996-7 season in which the club, with a ground holding just 3,500, finished tenth in the second division. Whilst not to the extravagant degree of Santiago Bernabeu fifty-four years earlier, Roig too set out with a clear vision. Within three years the stadium, El Madrigal, had been spruced up to accommodate 23,000, and Roig had pumped in all of £29 million to establish a youth academy. Meanwhile Villarreal had tasted life in the *Primera Division* for the first time – dauntingly, their opening fixture had been at the Bernabeu – but although demotion had been immediate, so too was a return to the top flight in 2000. Now, aided by a liberal supply of accomplished South Americans – Villarreal had smartly tapped into the Argentinian market particularly, and developed a home-from-home environment for them too – they began to earn plaudits for their eye-pleasing brand of play: 'we like our players to treat the ball well,' would say Francisco Garcia, a one-time coach. It was also a very effective brand of play. Inevitably there were hiccups along the way: Martin Palermo, so prolific in Argentina, failed quite miserably, while in early 2004 Benito Floro resigned as coach citing a poor attitude among the squad – 'It's now up to them to prove that I was the problem, not them.' And maybe he was, because after his departure Villarreal progressed to no less than the semi-finals of the UEFA Cup, where they lost only 0-1 on aggregate to seasoned Europeans and big-city neighbours Valencia. The following campaign, now under Chilean coach Manuel Pellegrini, they reached the quarter-finals – and finished marvellously third in *La Liga* too, walloping eventual champions Barcelona 3-0 at El Madrigal, thus qualifying for the UEFA Champions League. And, as we know, they did themselves so proud there, topping unbeaten their group that included Manchester United, eliminating Glasgow Rangers and Inter

Milan, and falling only 0-1 on aggregate to Arsenal in the semis, but missing a crucial last-minute penalty at home in the second leg when Lehmann saved Riquelme's kick.

Though the next season, and the current one too, had brought failure in Europe, Villarreal had followed up that third slot by finishing seventh then fifth, and were cementing further their place in the higher reaches now: prior to kick-off tonight, after twenty matches, they sat third in the table again.

Over the past few years their distinctive yellow shirts had been donned by the likes of – not to mention Reina, now between the sticks at Anfield – Sorin, Belletti (scorer of Barca's winning goal against Arsenal in that 2006 Paris final), Forlan (winner of the *Pichichi* in 2005) and indeed Juan Roman Riquelme, playmaking genius, aplomb incarnate, but an enigmatic character now back with Boca Juniors after his antics caused Villarreal's tolerance to run out.

For the club to accomplish what it has done, when only seventeen years ago it was plying its trade in front of just a hundred-odd onlookers and quite probably a mongrel dog with an irrigation fixation, is a fantastic achievement that shines ongoingly a torch for everyone.

O O O

Gate B was located in the south-west tower, one of four that made the Bernabeu look all the more theatrical. If the ascents of Wimbledon, Villarreal and indeed Getafe – themselves in the regional backwaters till 1986, still at the third level in 2002, but sitting twelfth in the *Primera* this morning – were fairytale, then mine now was mountainous. Having reached the near-summit, a kind young steward went beyond the call of duty to escort me up the final tortuous route to seat 10 on the next-to-back row of the topmost section of the west stand's *anfiteatro*: amphitheatre. Once more I was struck by the precipitousness of the tiering, and around me indeed were rails to prevent tumbling. There was half an hour to kick-off and the place was nowhere near full yet, so its layout was all the more discernible, tier upon tier, almost like some pale blue wedding cake, and yet for all its size there was somehow a sense of intimacy. That became more so fifteen minutes later when, feeling a sudden flush, I realised that a strip of electric heating installed in the roof had just been switched on and was all aglow. Some living room. And high up I was. The advertising balloon of Real's shirt sponsors, bwin.com, was floating around way beneath me.

With its current capacity of 80,000, the Bernabeu is around four-fifths the size of the Camp Nou, but once it had held much more, prior to its conversion to seats-only. In those heady days of the late fifties, it indeed looked different, not just with its terracing but also because the east stand had risen its extra tier above the rest of the bowl, and the place was roofless. Trying to imagine Kopa, di Stefano, Gento et al as they rose to the challenge of the Busby Babes wasn't straightforward, especially as that semi-final first leg back in April 1957 had been played in the afternoon, the Bernabeu at that time without floodlights. Yet, perched as I was now in these rafters of such a floodlit, modernised, monumentally levelled up setting, the aura genuinely remained with all of its evocation.

○ ○ ○

Seventy-five thousand attended tonight. The timing of such a formidable fixture was less than kind for Villarreal, sandwiched as it was between the two legs of their *Copa del Rey* quarter-final against Barca, the first having produced a goalless draw at El Madrigal three nights ago and the second only four nights away. No such complications for Real: their less than first string had already been eliminated by Mallorca, while their other priority was on-track, the first knock-out round of the UEFA Champions League to be dealt with not for a while yet.

I wanted to see for myself just what Villarreal were made of now. First, though, I struggled to see exactly who was turning out, for the video screens at each end that displayed the line-ups were half-obscured by my roofing. The free match brochure was of a somewhat generic nature, though it did set out the expected teams and, as it transpired, *Mediapunta* had it mostly right. Not, then, wholly.

I had a marvellous view, just to the right of the halfway line. It was marvellous in that the entire proceedings were set out before me; or, should that be, below me. Not only could I see every development of play, but also any potential development. A chess grandmaster with a love of football would have been both on familiar ground and intrigued: so long as he could pick out the pieces. I took out my binoculars. Real's players were confirmed in their recognition and no further checking there would be necessary. But it took me five minutes to determine that Robert Pires, due to be playing, wasn't; and I'd need to peek every now and again to confirm which visiting performer had done whatever. Among their faces unfamiliar to myself were Bruno and Cazorla who'd both graduated from that youth academy. Missing from their line-up tonight was Matias Fernandez, a youngster signed from Colo Colo as Latin America's newly named Footballer Of The Year for 2006: Villarreal's smartness continued.

Back in the second fixture of the campaign, following their own opening-day 3-0 dismantling of Valencia away, they'd been mauled 0-5 by Real at El Madrigal. Yes, I wanted to take a good look at Villarreal tonight.

So too did a hundred of their fans, tucked away in the topmost north-east corner of the stadium. Directly opposite me, meanwhile, were the coaches' and squads' benches, Capello's craggy features now replaced by Bernd Schuster's flowing locks, the Italian away to sort out England's malaise and the German fetched in from Getafe across the city to appease the aesthetes.

Curiously, away down to my right, the section for Real's notorious *Ultras Sur* – a hard-core, right-wing following with a history of violence – was less than full.

○ ○ ○

'*Illa, Illa, Illa, Juanito Maravilla*!!' came the chant after seven minutes. Sure enough, those *Ultras Sur* hadn't forgotten. Within a couple of minutes they had a goal to celebrate too, as Guti's sliderule pass found Robinho's dart into the box from the left and the Brazilian, taking advantage of some sleepy defending, shot unchallenged low past Diego Lopez' outstretched left arm. It looked likely that Real with their smart interchanging and swift passing were going to grip the game, but Villarreal stuck in there and, lo and behold, they equalised after fifteen minutes, their ex-Manchester United forward Rossi also left free inside the box to belt the ball into Casillas' top right corner. For the remainder of the first half it was mostly a case of Real's striving to make their greater possession count but Villarreal's refusing to buckle, although, whilst the visitors were playing cautiously, they certainly weren't being negative. They were fortunate in the thirty-fifth minute though when the referee ignored a valid penalty claim, van Nistelrooy barged in the back by the Uruguayan defender Godin as he went for a close-range header.

According to *Marca*, Real's possession in the first half had been sixty per cent, but the second half was virtually even in that respect, and this was '*un duelo de titanes*' with Villarreal '*un magnifico adversario*'. It certainly developed into a stirring contest. Robinho, in fine form tonight, scored again in the fifty-second minute, coolly despatching the ball low to the goalkeeper's left after a sweeping counter-attack had led to a bout of frantic blocking in front of goal. But Villarreal, made of stern stuff indeed, continued to lock horns and in the seventy-fifth minute they pulled level again. Maybe, with the benefit of my ultimate vantage point, I'd found myself being too judgemental: it's all so easy sitting in the stands, and who the hell am I? But more than just a few times I'd thought that the defenders of either team hadn't been switched-on enough, not alert to emerging danger. Usually it had been a case of failing to see the big picture, movement on their blind side, but Villarreal's second equaliser was different: unbelievably sloppy defending at a corner-kick. *Marca* would show a photograph of this. No less than nine Real players were well inside the area (two including Casillas on the goalline) but two Villarreal players were wholly unattended inside the six-yard box, and left-back Capdevila smacked the ball home.

Lluis had wondered how I'd find the atmosphere inside the Bernabeu. He told me he'd all too often found the Camp Nou, perhaps because Barca fans usually expect a home victory, to be rather quiet. Well, it might have seemed more noisily animated had I been lower down, more amongst it, but, yes, I found the Bernabeu to be rather quiet too on the whole, perhaps for the same reason. Those hundred-odd visiting fans were unsurprisingly audible in greeting their team's goals, but now and again, though immediately being drowned out by horn-blowing in the adjacent section, they were audible above the seventy-five thousand in other moments too.

Their celebration now was quickly muted not only by angry horns but by Real's third goal less than sixty seconds later. A smart pass by Gago found Sneijder, not long on for Baptista, and the Dutchman drilled the ball through Diego Lopez' desperate challenge from the left corner of the six-yard area, right in front of the *Ultras Sur* who probably thought that the rest of the crowd should make noise like theirs more often.

I wouldn't have enjoyed sitting behind or next to myself, given my constant fidgeting to pull out pen, paper and binoculars. I trained the latter not only on players' expressions but also off the park. Schuster was his often inscrutable self, Pellegrini betrayed some disgust, squad players were variously biting nails or picking noses either hunched forward or with feet up, but I tried to find the presidents, Roig and Calderon, now in his second season after Perez' resignation. I couldn't, and didn't try again because Villarreal were continuing to do their utmost, playing with real conviction.

The referee, Alvarez Izquierdo, had been getting some abuse, probably not least because he hailed from Barcelona. As the contest reached its climax, he provoked rage by going well beyond the displayed two minutes' stoppage time, but during this period Villarreal probably had greater cause for exasperation. They had a free-kick twenty-five yards out, central, from which Senna slipped a dangerously cute ball, angled right to unhinge a defence that once more had gone to sleep. Izquierdo called it back, but everything had seemed ready to me. The retake resulted in a corner – Villarreal's twelfth to Real's nine – but, nervousness filling the air, the team all in white prevailed; though Pellegrini would complain of a foul by Raul on Cygan leading up to their third goal.

For myself, aside from the fact that I'd witnessed a grandly absorbing match, another pleasing feature was the absence again of 'simulation'. Guti, very impressive in his playmaking here, indulged in his usual whingeing, but I saw no diving or feigning of injury. Indeed, only once did a player require attention, Salgado after all of eighty minutes, and he was substituted too. There'd been a fine spirit about the game.

I inched my way down the amphitheatre and, as the Bernabeu emptied, stood against a rail for a last reflective look around. I remembered a photo I'd seen recently of Santiago Bernabeu himself doing something similar; *Marca* had been carrying insertions, memorabilia collectively named *Los Tesoros* (treasures) *Del Real Madrid*, and there was the great man, in overcoat and trilby and holding a cigar, looking over Real's then ramshackle little ground back in 1943. My reality now had been his vision.

I had reasons to dislike Real Madrid. I spared a thought for poor, tragic Laurie Cunningham, killed in a car crash on the outskirts of Madrid in the summer of 1989, and recalled how dismayed I'd also been ten years before that when Real took his genius from us, our genuine chance of glory disappearing with him, oblivion awaiting us instead. Real, too, had been a prime component of G-14, that group of the self-considered elite who looked out only for their own interests and to hell with all the plebs. The most financially powerful club in the world – Deloitte put their total revenue for the 2006-7 season at £236 million – Real brazenly pursue commercial gain and indeed are representative of a playing field totally dislevelled today by money. Nottingham Forest won the European Cup inside the Bernabeu but they can't ever win it again, unless of course some multi-billionaire lands his helicopter by the Trent. And then there's Ferenc Puskas; though Real deny the accusations. He passed away in November 2006 after a long illness, the terrible Alzheimer's disease. The club attested that since September 2000 it had been sending a sum of money every month to Budapest to help his treatment, though that sum wasn't specified. But what we do know is that, when Real played a benefit game against a Hungary XI in August 2005, they claimed a match fee for themselves of £880,000 but raised just £62,000 for their old hero.

But I had reasons, too, to like Real Madrid. Of sentimentality, yes, for the name is synonymous still with the enchantment felt by that nine-year-old newly in love with football. And, yes, I had been charmed by them tonight also. It was with these good thoughts that I finally tore myself away from the inside of the Bernabeu, a theatre indeed. I suppose my visit, really, had been not too dissimilar in some respects to that of some gawping Japanese tourist to Old Trafford. But the experience that I'd just had, aside from being a wholly new one, had been a thoroughly enjoyable one as well. And, if I'm honest, it somehow felt too that, now, I'd really arrived in Spanish football.

○ ○ ○

'*Campeones*!! *Campeones*!!' came the cries outside, ignoring the fat lady. (Actually I now saw numerous fat ladies, and was quite surprised just how many whole families had been to the match.) This was Real's eighth league victory in a row but, more saliently than that statistic, Lilian Thuram had scored a late own-goal at the San Mames and Barcelona had thus only drawn with Athletic Bilbao earlier tonight. The gap at the top was now all of nine points.

As for Villarreal, they remained in third place, and later that night I came across a group of their supporters. I was in the Gambrinus bar near Tribunal metro station, watching the match highlights on its television, when suddenly through the window came the rather surprising sight of at least a dozen of them, all sporting colours. As they trooped inside I could see that there were three generations involved, so some of them would already have been well into their thirties as the team paddled around in those regional league backwaters. What a transformation these men had lived through. Sadly, the barman wouldn't serve them, but only because he was about to close, and no-one argued. When I duly stepped outside myself ten minutes later it felt good to know that they hadn't been spited, and I was also glad to have had the chance to tell them that their team was a fine one and to wish them all the best, meaning every word.

7

A FISTFUL OF EUROS

Sunday 16th March

There's a kind of intimacy about travelling by coach. An aeroplane will transplant you without regard for humankind below, changing landscapes paid no heed, sense of distance blurred. A train, whilst providing a sense of graduation, will stick to its iron straight and narrow. But a coach will weave its way unrigidly through that humankind, negotiating a congested little town centre here, past gawping faces, maybe nudging against some ravine there, and, unlike a train, there's a singularity about it: one coach. You feel more in tune with the terrain, the people, and the sense of journey. It touches the parts other modes of public transport cannot, and it's more of an adventure.

Such was my anticipation now on this Saturday morning as the local train clattered along its own straight and narrow to Malaga, from where I'd board an Alsina coach to Almeria: 220 kilometres but almost five hours through a landscape I'd yet to experience. For better or worse, I felt an uncertainty about it all too. Would there be room on the coach? I could've bought a seat on the internet but my printer had been in mischievous mode and, anyway, surely not everyone including octogenarians in Andalucia were online? Room on that coach, thankfully, there was. But, for at least those five hours, there would remain a fear that I'd be unable to get to the match. Almeria's stadium held only 22,000, you couldn't buy off their website, and on the Sunday evening their visitors were Barcelona. This was a match that I really did want to see. Almeria were making one hell of a good fist of surviving their first-ever season in the top division – six weeks earlier they'd beaten Real Madrid - and I wanted to see what made them tick. Barcelona? Hardly the worst attraction. I reclined my ridiculously inexpensive seat, rejoiced in the feeling that my knees were wholly unassailed by the furniture in front, watched Malaga's big-boat port and then its fledglingly marketed sand – 'The City With A Beach' – slide by; and I was away. With what turned out to be my very own personal guide, reclined next to me, Maria.

It was a cloudy day but the sun was insistent and warm through the coach's windows, the Mediterranean the other side of my own, mountains away to my left. Maria, tall and twentyish with curly long fair hair, was glad to be back, to see her parents and friends again. She'd returned to Andalucia ten days earlier than planned from her month away to learn English through a work-experience arrangement. It was with not a little incredulity that I listened to where she'd just been, reminding me of a long-ago moment when I'd been in a bus shelter in West Bromwich and an Italian tourist had sought Queen's English directions to Dudley Zoo. Maria – some arrangement – had just spent three weeks in – somehow – Cork. The pub hadn't been of the greatest assistance and the persistent rain had forever made everything worse. Thus it was now that she'd thought she'd practise on me: "I love to talk with people." She told me that she'd bought oranges in Cork that came from her home town; and she told me now, ten kilometres from Nerja, to look out for *plasticultura*. I'd already heard of this phenomenon, and here was my first view, almost like some African refugee camp: swathes of polythene tents housing forcibly produced fruits, vegetables and flowers, the canopies inducing tropical conditions, the irrigation drip-feed, modern technology enabling all kinds of preferred requirements to be met year-round, like peppers ready-holed for stuffing. But this was scant preparation for three hours later.

Some of the place-names inevitably echoed past fortification from would-be invaders: Torre del Mar. Others emphasised geography: La Herradura (The Horseshoe), as the coach twisted its way, including along tunnels, through an increasingly jagged, forbidding and spectacular mountainscape, before descending to cliffs' feet and sheltered living space. By this time we'd entered Granada province, and my self-displeasure at still not having got round to visiting that jewel of a city itself was assuaged by both the genuine pleasure of where the driver was taking me anyway and those innocent thoughts conjured up whenever I gazed, much beyond Maria, to my left. She'd noticed my making notes, including of something eventually revealed in its fulsomeness atop the hillside white town of Salobrena, another but startlingly imposing Moorish castle remnant. So why are you going to Almeria, she asked, then blew an air of heavy doubt at the likelihood of my getting a ticket.

At Motril the coach two-thirds emptied into a town of contrary grimness, a bit like coming across Middlesbrough after rolling through picturesque north Yorkshire to be met by chemicals and cranes. *Sin embargo* (that adopted phrase again), as we now honkingly manoeuvred for escape beyond double-parked vans and obstinate inner streets, a dastardliness of routing, I spied Calle Gerald Brenan. This commemorated the reclusive yet famed (in Spain, at any rate) English author of *South From Granada*, recounting his years spent nearby in the pre-Franco Alpujarras, an essentially rustic region of peaks, fertile valleys and simplicity in more ways than one, subsequently portrayed lovingly also by Chris Stewart's acclaimed *Driving Over Lemons*. Most evocative above all, though, and duly pointed out too by my companion who evidently knew her stuff, was the knowledge that twenty-odd miles inland from Motril lay the *Puerto del Suspiro del*

Moro: the Pass of the Sigh of the Moor. In 1492, the same year that Columbus would set sail from Huelva to discover the New World, and with the Inquisition already well under way to Catholicise a new unifiable Spain under its dual monarchs Fernando and Isabel, the last Muslim stronghold – the Kingdom of Granada – had surrendered. Boabdil, that last Moorish ruler, had turned at the pass on the fringe of the Sierra Nevada to take one final look at his beloved lost city. Perhaps he'd have been just slightly consoled had he known that, more than five hundred years afterwards, all over Andalucia, the Moorish legacy is inescapable.

Through Calahonda and Castell de Ferro, then on from Melicena where the driver's thirty-minute seafront break had enabled the pair of us to light up and Maria to also leg-stretchingly send chuckling words into her father's ear, winding beyond other small resorts like La Rabita, and then we reached Adra. The *Rough Guide* describes Adra, rather unfairly I think, as a 'place with non-existent charms'. I said farewell here to my fleeting friend, waved at her sitting on suitcase awaiting her dad, looked at the sparkling sea, and felt happy that she didn't have to live in Derby.

O O O

By now the landscape to my left was looking all the more parched, those mountains all the more craggy, brown and impossible. And then it hit me. Those earlier viewings had constituted but a modest foretaste, for here now was a whole stunning ocean of white plastic, stretching literally as far as the eye could see, which would indeed be the panorama from Poli Ejido's main stand. The town of El Ejido had seen its population burgeon over the past twenty-odd years from just a couple of thousand to more than fifty thousand, which didn't include the indigent occupants of those makeshift, wretched dwellings on its fringe, thousands of Africans who'd slipped their way here to eke out a dire living beneath the polythene; El Ejido, thus producing a billionaire or two also, is the hub of *plasticultura*. Bad feeling towards the slave-labourers simmers here – '*Inmigrantes O Andaluz?*' had been daubed heavily on a city wall – but their toiling has also been a factor in the rise of Poli Ejido, promoted from the *Tercera Division* in 2000, from the *Segunda Division B* in 2001 when their neat little new stadium was inaugurated, and thereafter consolidated at the second level: all achieved with *plasticultura* wealth. The current president, Gabriel Hidalgo Martin, was now in his eighth season at the helm and back in the summer he'd appointed a new coach, Luis Cesar Sampedro, who had a history of hauling clubs to promotion: Racing Ferrol to the second level in 2004 and Nastic to the top level in 2006. The intention went without saying but such ambition wouldn't be realised so smoothly. This very evening Poli Ejido would lose 0-2 at Cadiz, would find themselves at the bottom of the table by the end of the weekend, five points from safety, and Sampedro had already been replaced. Producing tomatoes the size of oranges was one thing, but having Real Madrid amid the plastic wasn't at all a ripe proposition. And although such intensive agricultural operation had invigorated Almeria province's impoverished economy, I must say that, after the initial breathtakingness, I'd found myself looking at without doubt the most hideous sight I'd yet encountered since leaving England.

○ ○ ○

Twenty-five minutes late, at ten past four, the coach pulled into Almeria city's terminus. The tardiness wasn't a concern as long as I could get a taxi quickly. A cluster of them indeed were waiting and I asked for the Estadio Juegos Mediterraneos. Among the things I'd gleaned from UD Almeria's website prior to setting out were that match tickets would already have been put on sale to the general public before my arrival, that the ticket office by the Preferencia Stand would reopen at half-past four this afternoon, and that the club was evidently making serious capital out of this fixture, as it doubtless would have done also for the visit by Real Madrid. For it appeared that a season ticket hadn't already bought entry: you were required to pay extra for Barcelona. However, season ticket holders were being charged half that price demanded of the general public. Put another way, I was being made to fork out double. Not knowing exactly where the stadium was, only assuming that it was on the fringe of town, I was relieved that the taxi took less than ten minutes to get me there, depositing me at the edge of a vast car park, which was practically empty. I was even more relieved to see just half a dozen men waiting for the ticket kiosk to open; this implied that there were tickets still available and also, given the absence of any queue, that there'd indeed be one for me. That said, I was still bracing myself, for I suspected that the less expensive ones had already been snapped up. At bang on four-thirty the shutters were rolled up to reveal three windows, all of them in use, and I actually became joint-first to be served.

Ten miles or so north of Almeria, Spain's hottest province and Europe's driest region takes on an especially harsh character, desert terrain where all is gnarled and hostile. *Lawrence Of Arabia* is one cinematic classic part-shot here, but this is famously Spaghetti Western territory: *A Fistful Of Dollars* and the rest. Well, for a few dollars more now, and a seat in the centre of the Tribuna Stand's upper tier, I might have spat out – get ready to drop that cheroot – three hundred euros. I asked, less in expectation and much more in almost risible hope, for a seat in the *Fondos* – behind the goal – which had been the cheapest available. The Old Man handed one over. I had the least expensive seat going. At the Bernabeu a few weeks earlier Real Madrid had cost me forty euros. UD Almeria were now taking ninety of my euros. My fist retained those other two hundred and ten I'd had ready. Thus the two hundred quid with which I'd lined the pockets of some big, fat, bald, ugly Yorkshire bastard in Osaka six years earlier remains the most I've ever spent to enter a football stadium.

Thus too I had enough money with which to treat myself now to a nice hotel, but settled anyway for the perfectly comfortable and quite inexpensive Hotel La Perla just off Puerta de Purchena, a city hub that featured a statue of Nicolas Salmeron, a late nineteenth century president of the First Spanish Republic, born in Almeria and looking here quite avuncular. Unfortunately and very disrespectfully in a city that, besides having straightaway seemed to look, well, blendingly light brown like its nearby mountains, had soon revealed too its rampant graffiti, someone had scrawled 'Black Sabbath' in black felt-tipped pen on his left shoulder. Unfortunately too, after a pleasant evening stroll and a most welcome dish of spaghetti bolognese, all the time congratulating myself upon a mission accomplished, I then walked into an internet cafe to be informed that Leicester City had won 4-1 at The Hawthorns. Thanks, Albion. Things might've been worse, though. Later I found myself in a heaving little bar named El Candil amid – though I had the benefit of a stool for both comfort and easy service – locals enjoying their balmy Saturday night's drinking and *tapas*, the bar staff performing wonders of perpetual motion while I watched Sevilla beating Valencia. My mobile blew off. Albion, although having reached the FA Cup semi-finals the weekend before, were currently wresting failure from the jaws of promotion, and the voice, belonging to a longstanding mucker of mine from Tividale with a penchant for bellyaching, was an inebriated but distinctly unhappy one. "Fuckin' racked off the Albion am," it said. "Where are you?" I asked. "In the Fox'n'Dogs an' ah'm fuckin' soakin', it's fuckin' pissin' down 'ere, ah'll tell y'. Wharra yo doin' now?" I gave him a description and effing well felt better.

○ ○ ○

Barcelona, too, might have been feeling slightly better on Sunday morning, for Real Madrid had slipped up again the night before, losing 0-1 at the Riazor against lowly Deportivo, their fourth defeat in seven league matches since their fans had assumed the title was already theirs after that victory against Villarreal. Still, though, the gap was eight points. Yet three weeks earlier Barca had whittled it down to just two after Eto'o's hat-trick had helped see off bottom-placed Levante and Real had lost 0-1 at the Bernabeu to plucky Getafe, whose winning goal had been a knife-through-butter breakaway as half a dozen Real players had been hugging themselves at the other end in celebration of a 'goal' of their own, disallowed for offside. But Barca had lost their last two league fixtures, 2-4 away to Atletico Madrid and then 1-2 at the Camp Nou against resolute Villarreal. *Marca* had wondered loudly whether anyone actually wanted to win this league.

These were certainly difficult days for Barcelona. Yes, they were now Spain's sole survivors in the UEFA Champions League, through to the quarter-finals – Real had been knocked out by Roma eleven days ago while the night before that Sevilla had heartbreakingly lost a penalty shoot-out to Fenerbahce at the Sanchez Pizjuan – but the camp was far from a well one. "He won't listen to me!" had laughed Hermo, who'd also been a coach and with whom I'd eventually and inevitably had a chat about football. But, any joking about filial disregard aside, Frank Rijkaard was now under ever increasing pressure, his decision-making in terms of both selection and tactics being criticised heavily by the press and interviewed fans alike, his likely successors after almost five seasons in charge being openly discussed. And there was evident unrest in the dressing-room. Back in December, Brazilian midfielder Edmilson had given vent in a television interview, accusing some of his team-mates of caring more about the trappings of success than about the actual bread-and-butter on the pitch. 'Two years ago,' he'd said, 'we won the league and the Champions League and everyone fought to the death. But now we lack the unity of a team and the unity of a family.' The personification of this lack of dedication, this malaise, was considered by all and sundry to be Ronaldinho. Despite scoring with a fantastic overhead kick in that defeat by Atletico on the first day of March – after which game Rijkaard had taken particular flak for leaving Messi on the bench for an hour – he'd been variously left out, substituted and dropped, forever looking sluggish amid tales of off-field partying, and furthermore giving the impression of not being bothered by any of it.

Ronaldinho hadn't travelled to Almeria, either. At lunch-time I leisurely pored through *Marca* which typically analysed to the hilt – over its first eleven pages, no less – Real's defeat; it also provided graphic images of Athletic Bilbao's goalkeeper Armando being hit in the face by a water bottle chucked at the Ruiz de Lopera, causing that game's abandonment (there's some real marksmanship among Betis' lunatic element, as Juande Ramos would know, but obviously someone had still failed to confiscate the bottle-top at the turnstile); and it enabled me to clue-up about the match I'd come to watch. And Ronaldinho – for whatever reason in his case – wasn't the only absentee, injury problems not for the first time this season exacerbating Rijkaard's troubles. If I'm totally honest I still felt, for all that he wasn't himself, disappointed that I wouldn't be seeing the Brazilian stellar one in the flesh tonight. But I felt much more miffed that the freakishly talented Messi wouldn't be on show; twelve days earlier he'd been crocked again as Barca saw off Celtic and was expected to be out for another six weeks. Among the nine players unavailable to Rijkaard now were also the Mexican defender Marquez, the Ivorian defensive midfielder Toure, the playmaker Deco and the teenaged Mexican forward for whom a bright future was predictedly in store, Giovani dos Santos, while the ex-Juventus right-back Zambrotta was suspended. Nevertheless Rijkaard was putting on a bullish front, insisting that the chase was still on and the belief was still there. '*El grupo trabaja bien y con mucha mentalidad*': Barca were focused and hard at it.

O O O

The history of Spanish club football is littered with *fusiones* and *refundaciones*. Whereas in England clubs have been identifiably rooted since the year dot (and nor would it be difficult to trace MK Dons' highly dubious lineage), Spain demands a bit of untangling, and Almeria provides another such confusing case.

Today was the fourth ever visit by Barcelona to this city: to play a third different entity. The records show that a club named Almeria spent two seasons in the top flight around the turn of the 1980s, drawing 1-1 then losing 2-5 at home to the visitors for whom a certain Bernd Schuster scored twice; but that club was Agrupacion Deportiva Almeria, which *Wikipedia* tells us disappeared in 1982. And then there'd existed a club named Polideportivo Almeria, which the *Marca* guidebook's historical section has disappearing no less than four times over seventy-odd years, though not without assuming AD Almeria's results along the way. In the 1999-2000 season Poli Almeria, then at the third level, had held their illustrious opponents to a goalless draw here in the *Copa del Rey*; and then only late goals by Xavi and Rivaldo had seen them off at the Camp Nou. Meanwhile, another team had been formed in the city in 1989: Almeria Club de Futbol. Although Paco Martin's book about the history of football in Fuengirola has opponents by the name of UD Almeria participating in group nine of the *Tercera Division* during the 1989-90 season (along with Poli Ejido and the forerunners of Malaga CF), other records have it that Union Deportiva Almeria were officially so christened on 28th June 2001 after the *fusion* of Almeria CF and Poli Almeria. For all this confusion, one thing strikes me: the *pueblo* element. Tonight I'd see men in their sixties shouting their proverbials off. The expressions on their faces told of a lifelong localised passion for football. So, because UD Almeria was (for argument's sake) only nineteen years old, they must also have shouted their knackers off for either AD or Poli in the past. Given too that for a dozen years or so CF and Poli had indeed been city rivals, their purple faces here surely proved that they were actually supporting their *pueblo* itself through the conduit of the football team now representing it. This, it seems to me, is a defining element of club support in Spain generally: pronounced local honour, rising up against the rest.

○ ○ ○

UD Almeria, besides being that example of confusing lineage, also provide another Spanish tale of heartwarming progression: and, more than that, of subsequently keeping heads above water. As recently as 2000 the club was still at the fourth level, but in 2007, despite having lost their opening three games of that season, they'd finished runners-up to Valladolid at the head of the second. Now, unlike Valladolid and Murcia who'd also come up with them, but who were both in the relegation places this morning, UD Almeria sat a healthy, fists-clenched eighth with thirty-seven points from twenty-seven matches. Whilst they'd certainly struggled to score goals – a paltry twenty-three so far – only Barca had conceded less, and the team was grinding out sufficient results through an uncomplicated brand of play that, without being negative, was fundamentally guarded yet fiercely combative, loose balls contested for all they were worth. Nowhere more so had their marvellous work ethic been displayed than on the first weekend of February when Real Madrid had come to Almeria and lost 0-2, the home side full of self-belief, totally unfazed by celebrities who may have been more than a tad presumptuous. Among others seen off here had been Espanyol and Sevilla, whilst on their travels Almeria's achievements had included victories at Deportivo and Valencia and a draw at Villarreal.

Right now, though, they were suffering injury problems of their own. Bruno, the right-back, was sidelined with an ankle knock; Acasiete, a defender with twenty-one caps for Peru and who'd started out with the curiously named Deportivo Wanka, and Paunovic, the Serbian forward who'd played for Mallorca in the last ever Cup-Winners' Cup Final and managed to get sent off on his debut at Santander three weeks ago, were also absent; Corona, the influential central midfielder, was a major doubt. The latter had spent the previous season on loan from Zaragoza but during the close-season had made his transfer permanent, and in that past summer Almeria had indeed brought in several new players to help consolidation in the top flight, whilst several others – including Sander Westerveld, the ex-Liverpool goalkeeper – had been shown the door. Among those arrivals were Diego Alves, a young 'keeper from Atletico Mineiro; Aitor Lopez Rekarte, the experienced full-back from relegated Real Sociedad; Felipe Melo, a Brazilian central midfielder from Racing de Santander; Julio dos Santos, a young Paraguayan international midfielder on loan from Bayern Munich where opportunities had been sparse; and Alvaro Negredo, a big raw-boned centre-forward also on loan, who'd banged in eighteen goals for Real Madrid's B-team the previous season. Nor had they been idle during the January transfer window, during which only five Spanish clubs had spent any money at all: Almeria had splashed out one and a half million euros on the Brazilian wide midfielder Guilherme from Vasco da Gama.

Diego Alves had just been called up for the first time by Brazil for a forthcoming friendly against Sweden, an honour for his new club which unsurprisingly had yet to either provide a player for the Spanish national team or win a trophy. The dissimilarity to Barca could hardly have been greater, but this contest tonight, all things considered, promised to be an absorbing one.

○ ○ ○

Kick-off being at 7pm, *Marca* digested, I had time still to spend before making my way to the stadium, and on the subject of absorption the city of Almeria had done much soaking up over the years. Aside from its Moorish past – the huge Alcazaba castle that bestrides the place is the next largest such edifice in Andalucia after Granada's renowned Alhambra – it had suffered numerous violent earthquakes during the sixteenth century, while in 1937 it was actually shelled: by Hitler's navy. Staunchly Republican during the Civil War, Almeria would become one of the last cities to fall to Franco, long after his fascist ally with the mad eyes and silly little moustache had tried to intimidate it. But for all its trials and tribulations, the city today, under another clear blue sky, looked essentially smart, though in its rundown Chanca area I saw an urchin or three amid unpaved backstreets, gypsy music in the air. I also saw, back in Puerta de Purchena, a chap in his fifties all by himself sporting a Barca scarf: time to go.

The stadium, part of a sports complex run by the municipality, had cost twenty-one million euros to build in 2004. In February 2005 it had staged a World Cup qualifier against San Marino but, as its name signifies, it was constructed primarily to stage the fifteenth Mediterranean Games that summer, a mini-Olympics whose hosting would help put an ambitious city on the map. The football team now using it was helping in that respect still more. Of uniform grey steel, I wouldn't describe it as a characterful place, though it certainly had a few distinctive features. Aside from its four floodlight pylons, huge capital Hs that tilted inwards, the roofed bowl was largely backless; as the match would progress and sunlight succumb to floodlight, it'd feel very unusual indeed to see the city's own distant lights in between the roof and the top row of heads. Plus, I struggled to recall any other football ground I'd been to that had landscaped gardens by its turnstiles.

My arm-and-a-leg seat in the *Fondo Norte Bajo*, near the front (ie the bottom), afforded a close sight of the running track this side of the right corner flag: not the best view I'd ever had. We quickly get used to that, though, don't we? And I was in the same end as Almeria's main mob, too: good.

○ ○ ○

Corona was fit and took his place while, for Barca, Thierry Henry was left on the bench. Without in the slightest wanting to disparage this particular Frenchman – Arsenal's record goalscorer, for goodness' sake – one could see the wisdom of the very astute Wenger, who was by now constructing yet another fine team (albeit virtually non-English), one that was perhaps liberated by the departure of an erstwhile talisman now facing his twilight years. Nor, then, was Henry a fixture in Barcelona's eleven, assimilation into that structure proving difficult, amid wider accusations that Barca themselves of late had erred into their own '*galacticos*'-equivalent, big names fetched in but something lost along the way. The visitors' focal attacker tonight was Samuel Eto'o for whom, injury-plagued of late, this was his hundredth league game in Barcelona's colours, and who, in a press conference a couple of months earlier, had declared that the team ought to learn how to win ugly, if that was what winning called for.

There was a minute's respect paid prior to commencement, marked in typically Spanish fashion by mournful music, Almeria's players motionless in their starting positions while Barca's linked arms. Rijkaard's sidekick Johan Neeskens had just lost his brother following a long illness and Monday's *Marca*, with its penchant for graphics, would show a very emotional couple in the dug-out, Rijkaard genuinely so, face pained, arm around his mucker. As I gazed around I saw that Almeria hadn't quite sold all their tickets – there were a few empty seats on the lower sides close to each corner flag towards my end – and I also saw a banner imploring Almeria's coach not to leave: '*Unai, Almeria Te Necesita*!!'. Unai Emery, having just got Almeria promoted in his first season at the club, steering them now evidently in further progress, and still aged only thirty-six, was being coveted.

Within four minutes of the opening whistle I was aghast to

see two instances of something that, although I'd barely witnessed it myself since, had troubled me as an idea upon leaving England. Almost in front of me, Iniesta, for whom I've held much admiration, blatantly dived. Three minutes later Melo, coveted already by Fiorentina, lost possession in the centre-circle and blatantly dived. Neither were punished by the referee. Nicely, there were two sequels to this opening disappointment. More importantly, and gladly, nothing quite as bad happened again. And before too long the ref, Rubinos Perez, would get in the way of Lilian Thuram's sliding challenge; while Thuram, despite his own thirty-six years, would smoothly reconvene himself to glide onward, Perez struggled somewhat to raise himself from his backside, to universal glee around me. By that time Barca had snatched a lead, Iniesta's piledriver being spilled by Diego Alves after seventeen minutes and the teenaged prodigy Bojan ramming home the rebound. Cue interesting scenes in the *Fondo Norte*.

I'd seen Barcelona in the flesh once before, the 1992 European Cup Final at Wembley, when they'd made a point of changing into their true colours to receive the trophy. Now, half a dozen people a few rows directly below me, a handful of blokes and a couple of women all in their twenties, none of them conspicuously sporting colours, displayed their true allegiance. They shot up to cheer Bojan's goal. I also heard a sudden roar, maybe twenty- or thirty-strong, from somewhere behind to my left, presumably from one of the small separate sections forming the top of the stand. This induced a hundred or more home fans to leap to their feet, turn around, and shout abuse. Meanwhile, a couple of rows below to my right, a man in his sixties, bespectacled, baseball-capped and dripping with Almeria's red and white, stood in the gangway and hurled his own very loud diatribe over my head. This *pueblo* wasn't taking kindly to its being infiltrated. But whilst that small group below now resumed its low profile, I didn't notice any worried faces among them.

No-one was going to harm them, for I sensed no threat of physical violence in the air; this was merely a verbal outpouring, nothing more. There were probably twenty-odd security men with batons inside the stadium, and they stood motionless on the running track. Two policemen continued to amble together around that track. I was aware of no stewards or any other officials becoming involved. I'd seen one young steward in my vicinity and that gangway abuse-hurler in his sixties was left entirely to it. Nobody had overstepped any mark. I saw females young and old – and there were many here tonight – actually chuckling. Yet again inside a Spanish football ground I was struck by the total absence of jobsworths and their obsessions with 'safety' and their own self-importance.

In the thirty-second minute Almeria's fans had something more positive to shout about – though cue another turn around en masse and a urine-taking ditty – for their team equalised. From Barca's point of view it was an awful goal. Corona took a corner-kick on the right and centre-back Pulido, unbelievably in yards of space at the near post, flicked a header across 'keeper Valdes. Pulido hadn't even jumped, he'd simply trotted upfield for a free nod.

Though Barca looked individually more accomplished – perhaps epitomised in this first half by left-back Abidal's sublime foot control of an awkwardly spinning ball, plucking it out of the air, whilst a few moments later his counterpart Mane would laboriously require three touches to do something similar – Almeria were typically playing with high energy and admirable confidence, backed by marvellously vociferous (and drums-assisted) support, one that loudly protested everything too. It was an intriguing clash of styles, Barca with Rijkaard's favoured 4-3-3 attempting (not very successfully, for they did look distinctly out of sorts) to play their slick game, and Almeria with Emery's 4-1-4-1 playing robustly, intensely and more directly, Negredo a handful up front. Yet the home side were much more than just big hearts, and in Melo they had a particularly smooth operator within their orderly game plan.

There was a curious start to the second half, Barcelona's players out early and waiting for Almeria's to re-emerge, then Thuram's disappearing back into the dressing-room and ultimately keeping everybody waiting. It wasn't clear whether the visitors had received a flea in their ear from Rijkaard, or whether Emery had engaged in a spot of gamesmanship, or both; or whether, indeed, Thuram was making some point of his own. Before the night was over there'd come a moment when Thuram, who earlier in his long and distinguished career had been arguably the best defender in the world, would go missing again in a more serious way.

Barca began the second period by keeping the ball better and, just nine minutes into it, made their first substitution: enter Henry, replacing the defensive midfielder Edmilson, not the most popular in the dressing-room since his public outburst. This too allowed Iniesta to slot back into a customary midfield role having spent the first half on the left of Eto'o. Henry's impact was immediate and dramatic, dribbling in from the left and along the byeline to set up Eto'o to restore Barca's lead. Now, although their workrate would never drop, Almeria – and, to some extent, their fans also – would be somewhat quelled as the visitors showed more composure and authority. Not for that long, though. If the home side had already illustrated how solid and well-drilled they were – and their clutch of new signings had obviously bedded in sweetly – they now displayed resilience. They were, however, dealt a helpful hand.

Eight minutes after Eto'o's goal, Emery made a first substitution of his own, like-for-like in more ways than one: the right midfielder Juanma Ortiz was replaced by another right midfielder, Jose Ortiz, a long-serving player who was also the club captain. The latter provided more zip on that flank and within seven minutes of coming on he was instrumental in Barca's being reduced to ten men. This sending-off looked harsh to me. Ortiz burst up the right and the Argentinian centre-back Gabriel Milito was forced to come across. Near the edge of the box he made a sliding tackle, a genuine attempt to win the ball. A split second before Milito got there, Ortiz had poked the ball forward: too far by the look of it. Ortiz saw Milito's outstretched leg and thus opted to fall over it. Milito had already received a yellow card a quarter of an hour earlier, and now he was given another. Unsurprisingly he was incensed by the decision, taking some time to depart the field, turning back to complain to the referee yet again, before finally trudging off at a pronounced dawdle. Now I found myself remembering John Aldridge who famously admitted that during his time with Real Sociedad he'd bothered to learn only one phrase of Spanish. '*Hijo de puta*!! *Hijo de puta*!!' reverberated the invective aimed at the ambling Argentinian. ('Son of a whore!!')

Not only was the crowd fired up again now but also obviously the numerical advantage infused Almeria with renewed vigour, and Barcelona now had to really dig in, Rijkaard's pre-match insistence up for proving. Bojan was sacrificed, the ex-Arsenal player Sylvinho coming on at left-back and Abidal slotting in for Milito. Monday's *Marca* – Madrid-oriented, after all – would be rather scathing of Barca, describing them as '*sin alma*' (soulless), but I thought they did show good spirit in the final quarter of an hour, none more so than Eidur Gudjohnsen who continued to work his socks off.

But Barcelona's hopes of clawing three points nearer to Real were undone with five minutes to go, and once more it was a corner-kick met by a totally free header. This kick was from Almeria's left and thus I had a close view of what happened. Corona, again, took it. Thuram was concentrating more on his near-post wrestling bout with Negredo than on the real issue. The pair teetered and the ball escaped both of them overhead. The Nigerian centre-forward Kalu Uche, who'd come on as a sub five minutes earlier, leaped all alone to ram the ball to Valdes' left, before launching into a somersault celebration as those few visiting fans became subjected to greater derision.

Almeria really had the bit between their teeth now but Barca's ten men hung on for a point, which was one more than Real had managed here but two less than the requirement: with ten games left, the gap at the top of the table was now seven. Despite Real's own stuttering, there seemed all the more an air of inevitability about the destination of the championship; all the more, too, an inevitability of big changes at the Camp Nou come the summer.

As someone well acquainted with survival struggles – and failure – in England, I had to applaud Almeria, for they looked to be setting about their task in exemplary fashion. They were by no means safe just yet; below its upper reaches, the league table was currently so compressed that only seven points separated Getafe now in eighth from Recreativo in eighteenth, and thus Almeria, whilst now occupying ninth slot, were only six points above the trapdoor. Statistics? Almeria's victories tally was already in double figures, something that half the division had so far failed to achieve. They had one of the best defensive records, including twelve clean sheets. They were strong at home, nor so bad away – defeats on their travels numbering less than those matches from which they'd acquired points. But leaving statistics aside, they came across as a side destined for, at the very least, safety. The work ethic didn't involve chasing around like headless chickens. They didn't play with fingers crossed. They looked to be organised and motivated brilliantly by Unai Emery, each player knowing exactly what was expected of him and comfortable with that. Unlike Barcelona tonight who'd conceded two criminal goals, Almeria was a team that kept mistakes at the back to an absolute minimum. They were strong, trembled in the face of no-one (in their very first game of the season they'd gone to La Coruna and won 3-0), and gave their all for the whole ninety minutes. They competed, and with no little polish or threat. Tonight they'd had seventeen attempts at goal compared with Barcelona's eight, and forced eight corners to Barca's five. And nor did they compete dirtily. Not one of their players was carded tonight and, when Gudjohnsen was substituted two minutes into stoppage time, it'd been the first and only occasion in the entire match that anyone had required treatment.

Stepping through the countless monkey nut shells littering the deserted stadium – not red-seated, but blue to reflect the Mediterranean and its Games of three years ago – I came away feeling sure that Almeria would be fine. But whether Emery would still be there next season was less certain. As for Barca....

I wouldn't have said so to Lluis in Bar Gloria, but I couldn't feel sorry for Barcelona's fans right now, and in any case their team might still have ended up as this season's champions of Europe, which of course would be a huge finger in Real Madrid's eye. It's just that I can't find sympathy for those whose team is forever in for the big prizes and furthermore expect to win them. Expectation has never sat with me. I empathise only with those who live merely in hope, especially if that hope is usually a frustrated one. Tonight I felt pleased for Almeria and its supporters.

○ ○ ○

My time remaining in Almeria wouldn't be without its curiosities. Having been surprised by the sight of seven or eight police wagons – idle, I hasten to add – parked outside the stadium, I then found myself the sole passenger on a bus for the thirty-minute, traffic-delayed journey back into the city centre. "There will be special free buses after the match," my taxi driver had said. Being the sort of person who chooses, a bit like Boabdil perhaps, to take a last lingering look at certain places, and having also felt the need to make notes among the nut shells while things were still fresh in my mind, I'd resigned myself to walking back. Lo and behold, though, one last bus sitting empty in solitude save for its female driver and a male supervisor standing outside it smoking. I felt quite privileged, despite being charged.

Almeria had already come across to me as a kind of young people's city. On Saturday night I'd seen very many of them out on the town, including teenaged girls made up to the nines with thighs somewhat tartily on full view, and there'd been clubs aplenty to cater for them. I'd even seen a wannabe competition, the music blaring open-air on the main street, the Paseo de Almeria, temporary seating erected along it. Now, though, those seats were chock-full, and for a very different reason, and so were surrounding streets. The most eye-catching figures on view were those dressed in cloaks and Ku Klux Klan-like tall pointed hoods, part of inching processions accompanied by dirges and which featured painstakingly ornate floats. The sinister-looking figures were actually enacting penitence. All across Andalucia, this was now *Semana Santa* – Holy Week. Apart from marvelling at the spectacle, my first witnessing of such celebration (though I'd enjoyed countless *ferias* and *fiestas*), and marvelling at those hundreds if not thousands of all generations thronging the pavements in almost totally silent respect, and aside too from its being so boldly underlined to me just how seriously this country indeed took its religion, I felt, simply and undoubtedly, well and truly, in Spain. This became emphasised all the more at gone one in the morning when, whilst I chose now to get some kip, families were still eating and drinking at alleyway tables. Very different to drying out sorrowfully in The Fox And Dogs.

O O O

Whilst *Marca* showed a photograph of Carles Puyol – actually, because of his utter commitment, a hero of mine – trudging away bare-chested and head bowed, Monday's *La Voz de Almeria* plastered across its front page another telling image, Uche in the background on the point of going into orbit but Iniesta in the foreground looking as though he'd just done nine-tenths of a twenty-kilometre walk only to be disqualified for lifting. Unai Emery spoke of being pleased that his team had kept their mental strength to the last, but of being disappointed that they hadn't achieved their objective, which had been to win; Emery's positive thinking was surely another major factor in Almeria's vibrant progress. For their own parts, unsurprisingly, Rijkaard and technical secretary Txiki Beguiristain lamented in particular the failure of experienced players to do better at set-pieces (another well-known Almeria forte). Surprisingly, the official attendance figure was put at 18,605, some two and a half thousand less than had come to the Real Madrid game, while at least a couple of thousand less than it'd looked to me. Still, though, five thousand or so above the usual gate. Yet, for all that Almeria usually drew a crowd which only two-thirds filled the Juegos Mediterraneos, this still seemed, unlike for example Santiago de Compostela, like a football town to me. The club's badge was indeed emblazoned across it, while those fourteen thousand or so who habitually took themselves to the games were mostly both resplendent of the colours and rabid of support. I really hoped it'd all carry on.

A fistful of euros? Back in Fuengirola, Barry runs a weekly sweep. Anything to draw punters in. I've often wondered whether the sign outside D's Bar that states 'Barry, ex-Tavern, here every night from 6 – 12 except Tuesdays' actually keeps them out. The sweep involves correctly guessing the scorelines of one English match and one Spanish match. Nobody ever wins. Some of the ongoing dosh goes into some kitty for Christmas or charity or whatever, while the three hundred euros prize remains stagnant. It'd never entered my head throughout my time away. But now I discovered that my guess of Manchester City two, Tottenham one, had been a correct one. And that I'd put Barcelona to win 2-1. Had their experienced players done better at a set-piece just five minutes from time, my entire trip would have been paid for.

- "You haven't lost three hundred euros because you never had them in the first place," said Angela in her typically matter-of-fact way.

True enough.

8

RIVER DEEP, MOUNTAIN HIGH

Sunday 20ᵗʰ April

No coach journey this time, for I was travelling literally the length of Spain. Inevitably, as I approached the departures hall of Malaga's airport, I thought of the previous occasion I'd flown from here: just two weeks earlier for Albion's FA Cup semi-final, when we were cheated big-time, a blatant hand-ball playing a crucial role in the only goal. The painful memory of that trip was provoked all the more by the knowledge that my destination now was connected directly to Portsmouth by a boat service: Bilbao.

When I'd asked people if they'd ever been up there and, if so, how they'd found it, the replies invariably had been uncomplimentary – 'Well, it's a port city....'. The word 'dump', it seemed, fell just short of being aired. Meanwhile, a friend who'd left her 1999 edition of *Lonely Planet* with Angie had scrawled 'shit-hole' at the start of the Bilbao section. As my flight wasn't scheduled to land until knocking ten o'clock on the Saturday night, I'd prudently pre-booked a hotel room over the internet. Having done so, I browsed through a customer comment or two. The very first one had said that its location was terrible and she'd felt unsafe walking back there at night.

Bilbao, here I came.

○ ○ ○

The taxi driver had his radio tuned in to a match commentary as he ferried me from the bus terminus at Plaza Moyua, and I recognised the name 'Corona'. His demeanour hadn't seemed the most personable at first but yet again the universal popularity of football had provided conversation, and he confirmed that the match was Almeria's visit to Sevilla. Given that soft spot of mine for Sevilla but also my admiration for their visitors, I wasn't sure how I felt when he told me that Almeria were one-up. I was, though, quite relieved that he spoke in Spanish. For the whole of my two days here I would come across no-one, except the bloke on the hotel desk, who spoke English. So I'd need to summon up all the Spanish I'd taken on board. I hoped that this taxi driver was going to prove the norm. Had he spoken in *Euskara*, the language of the Basques, I'd have been in a spot of bother.

Duly checked into the two-star Hotel Vista Alegre that took its name from the nearby bullring, I ventured out, though not far. This wasn't because of any uneasiness about the location, which looked quite all right to me, but because there was a bar across the deserted street. It was what I'd call, despite my now being indeed in the Basque Country, a typically Spanish little bar, intimate and earthy, ankle-deep in the accepted practice of dropping your tissues to the floor after scoffing your snacks and depositing your fag ends likewise, though only a couple of middle-aged customers now were left. The television was on, its pictures were coming live from the Sanchez Pizjuan, and unbelievably Almeria were now 4-0 to the good. Kanoute would pull a solitary goal back and, from my vantage point of the stool nearest the screen, I'd also see that the white handkerchiefs were out at the Camp Nou after Barca's goalless draw with Espanyol.

○ ○ ○

Belying the forecast of heavy rain – which was what I'd left behind on the Costa del Sol – I awoke to sunshine streaming through my window out of a virtually clear sky: perfect for exploring the city prior to tonight's match.

Santiago de Compostela, with its verdant landscape and wet climate, its mystique and low energy, had held an air very different to that of any other place I'd been to in Spain. As I stepped out now, Bilbao's own aura immediately began to impact upon me, not in any jolting way as might a first sight of some spectacular waterfalls, for example, but in a seeping kind of way, your senses gradually filling up as might a bowl under a dripping tap. Bar signs, shop signs, bank signs in *Euskara*; folk shouting greetings across the street likewise; the odd old boy in black beret. And, at virtually every turn, and this in a major city, high green wooded hills visible on the close horizon. More than anything else, I'd feel, it was that which gave Bilbao both singularity and intimacy, which in turn doubtless fuelled something of which I'd be left in no doubt by the time I'd depart: pride, both civic and regional.

Basquedom, at a stroke, is a concept that engages, baffles, but, for some of those who are its non-activists, can be tiresome to say the very least. The very first time I'd entered Spain, all those years ago, had been through Irun: a night train en route to Alicante via Madrid, eyes sleepy, windows black. But my return journey had been in daylight and, in my albeit mid-twenties' naivety, not least where politics were concerned, I'd thought I could understand why some Basque people wanted not to be part of a Spanish lump. I'd just been clattered across an endlessly parched landscape but now, here, was a particular region of lush greenery, streams and mountains that were inviting instead of forbidding, nature at its nicest. In that naivety of mine, I'd thought that Basques felt separate due mainly to mere geography and its attendant historical emotion. Maybe some so do, but there are more fundamental reasons why Basques, more than any other regional peoples of modern Spain including Catalans, may feel different: a couple that have floated through the heavy mists of time, and another, felt especially by the separatists, whereby they've been cheated big-time.

English, with all of its vagaries, must surely be a language not easy to master by foreigners. Hungarian, so I've been told, is yet by far the most difficult of European tongues to grasp, its linguistic foundation based upon none this side of Asia except for, surprisingly and somehow, its having a similar root to Finnish. But – and for all that the tongues of Hungary and Finland are acknowledgeably different (and of course their users recognised as having state identities) – the Basque language is totally unique. It has no connection whatsoever to any other root. It is, structurally, both wholly unborrowed and wholly unlent. And it has been a way of communication in these parts for at least three thousand years. But it isn't only linguists who've found this neck of the woods engaging and baffling. Anthropologists have found much to get their teeth into as well. Basques are of a blood grouping different to the rest of Europeans' – with at least double the normal frequency of rhesus negative – and a school of thought actually has it that they are the last surviving representatives of the continent's aboriginal inhabitants, such theory borne out by comparing their current skull configuration with that of Paleolithic man from eleven thousand years ago. Little wonder that they consider themselves a race apart.

And then there are the *fueros*. Historically, self-determination has been a concept jealously guarded in the Basque Country. Neither the Romans nor the Moors could nail its isolated people down. Dating back to the twelfth century, those *fueros* documented the already age-old precepts by which the Basques had managed their own affairs. When, in the early sixteenth century, all the Basque provinces became part of the new, Catholic, unified Spain, a kingdom ruled from Madrid, they were allowed to retain their *fueros* as a measure of autonomy. These arrangements were duly respected for more than three and a half centuries. But, in 1876, upon the conclusion of a particularly vicious second Carlist War, a new constitution took delight in abolishing them. Things in the Basque Country were about to take a turn.

○ ○ ○

Whichever turn I took myself now, Bilbao's central area was most definitely no dump. The port area, true, was some distance away, but so too must have been any chimneys, belching or not, that had survived the city's regeneration following the demise of much of its traditional and heavy industrial base towards the end of the twentieth century. There was, for example, a large and most agreeable park, fountained, next to the Museo de Bellas Artes. I spent an idyllic couple of hours strolling or sitting alongside the Nervion river, among hundreds of Sunday promenaders, the river neither looking nor smelling in the least polluted any more. On this west bank of which stood the greatest emblem of the city's recent reinvention and hopeful revitalisation, an art museum whose enormous titanium structure is surely in itself one of the most imaginative sculptures ever – a design, spectacularly faithful to Bilbao's maritime history, somehow representing both the hull of a ship and the body of a fish: the Guggenheim. It was that imaginativeness which struck me secondly. In all honesty, and for all that I fully understood how the city was striving to redefine itself, and for all its proximity to water too, my first thought had been how incongruous it looked; but then the Guggenheim's architectural innovativeness was such that it'd doubtless appear incongruous whatever its setting. Plus – and this I must confess (though each to his or her own) – I'm probably something of a philistine where art's concerned anyway. I've stood in front of the Mona Lisa and thought her not enigmatic at all but simply fat and rather smug-faced. When I went several years ago to Florence to watch Albion, I came back out of the Uffizi within twenty minutes. Now, I imagined some builder of like mind saying to his mate here eleven years ago: 'Bloody hell, Javier, where's this bit supposed to go now?' Oh well.

The museum I'd really wanted to visit during my stay was the Vasco in the city's old quarter, the *Casco Viejo*, an area of narrow streets, charming architecture and countless little bars. The Vasco's exhibits charted Basque history and illustrated Basque culture, but sadly I discovered too late that it was shut not only on Sundays after two o'clock but also all day on Mondays. The Guggenheim had been pulling them in though and, just after midday, as I'd sat outside it chewing on an inordinately priced cheese cob (and Bilbao is indeed one of the most expensive cities in Spain), I'd espied a recognisable figure or three among a particular dozen-strong group. The face I'd noticed first belonged unmistakably to the German goalkeeper Timo Hildebrand, he of the flowing blond locks, and then I'd picked out the Brazilian midfielder Edu, formerly of Arsenal, and then I'd gazed at Nicola Zigic, the Serbian centre-forward so tall that the sky was doing him a favour by being cloudless. I've become somewhat puzzled by Valencia where colours are concerned. The official club crest, presided over curiously by a wings-spread bat, is yellow and red stripes, and such had been the shirts worn at The Hawthorns by Mario Kempes and the rest and indeed those featured on posters advertising the first leg of that long-ago UEFA Cup pairing in Spain – where Valencia had nevertheless worn all-white. Subsequently they settled upon black for their shorts. Their latter-day change strip, though, has usually featured not yellow and red striped shirts but plain orange ones. Now, for their midday stroll, these uniform tops weren't yellow, red, white, black or orange: they were blue. Which, despite what had taken place four days ago, was probably how the coach Ronald Koeman was feeling today.

By five o'clock my city exploring had left me feeling, well, lost. I'd crossed the river out of the *Casco Viejo* by its San Anton bridge and, after several minutes of putting my best foot forward, realised that both feet had delivered me only into some district that held no likelihood of signposting the correct way towards my hotel, buildings fast thinning out save for some housing estate across some green expanse before me. Fortunately, a taxi happened along. Now, in the safety of its front passenger seat, I entered an area that I'd have given a wide berth to in daylight never mind darkness. A subsequent look at the map told me that this would have been part of the San Francisco quarter, close to the Abando train station, a red-light district and teeming now with Arab-looking men and black youths, most of them looking harsh upon mean streets amid the slum.

But that aside, I'd found central Bilbao smart enough, its riverside picturesque, its old quarter particularly evocative, its streets largely clean, its ambience engaging, and its regenerative process evidently making good headway.

○ ○ ○

A light shower surprisingly greeted me when I stepped back out at 7pm, two hours prior to kick-off. Inside a small bar just off a street named after Simon Bolivar, the champion of South American independence who was born in these parts, I had my first real view of *pelota*, or its traditional Basque version anyway, the television showing two men engaging in a strange kind of long-range, bare-handed squash match. The bar – not so far from the stadium – wasn't very busy at all, but I was still quite surprised by an absence there of something that had been in my face at regular intervals throughout the day: an allegiance to Athletic. My earlier riverside amble had met with several kids, both boys and girls, aged anything from four upwards, wearing the shirt. I'd also come across a group of three middle-aged couples all of whom, including the women, were wearing red and white scarves at as early as two-thirty that afternoon. Those bars in the old quarter had been dripping with red and white striped shirts.

And then, as I turned back onto Simon Bolivar, and as would be the case too on other bar-plentiful streets leading up to the ground, here were those shirts again: all over the place. Facing the East Stand with its huge club badge was a whole row of drinking-holes, all overflowing with the colours, including some imaginatively oversized berets. Without a doubt, during my time in Spain thus far, this was both the largest concentration of bars in the vicinity of a football stadium and the biggest profusion of people flying the flag that I'd yet encountered. To say that this was a well-loved club would be somewhat off the mark. As befits a club whose home is nicknamed 'The Cathedral', I got the distinct impression that it was worshipped.

Inaugurated in August 1913, San Mames had indeed taken its name from a nearby church (legend has it that the lions refused to harm Mames when the Romans threw him to them), but the stadium's ecclesiastical pet name stems from an awestruck testimonial paid it by a correspondent attending its grand opening. Yet, and sad though this might sound, even heretical too, I've got to say that it now looked a bit on the tatty side. I'd noticed when buying my ticket that morning how parts of the exterior could have done with a serious sprucing up, the concrete blotched, the main grandstand appearing more than a tad neglected, the celebrated steel arch that bestrode the main stand revealing signs of rust too, the overall impression one of unaddressed wear and tear. For such an immensely proud club, I found this surprising. But, even though the river was little more than a stone's throw away, this wasn't The Riverside; San Mames had a distinctive face all right.

I took my seat a good half-hour before the opening whistle, a pricey one (fifty-five euros) high up in the East Stand, and cast both eye and mind. The former was a much more pleasurable experience than that of a fortnight before. I hate the new Wembley. Quite aside from its rip-off catering and its rip-off match programmes (another free one here at the San Mames, by the way), and leaving out that it took the whole of half-time to take a leak (four sentried ladies' toilets in my area, virtually unused, but just one gents', and that the size of a pea pod), it's totally devoid of character; like all too many new stadia, its design precludes evocation. Its giant arch, eulogised by many, just smacks to me of an architect's ego trip. They said keeping the twin towers (and keeping the players' tunnel at one end might just have helped a bit too) was troublesome. Well, when they redeveloped the San Mames for the 1982 World Cup finals, its much-loved and much more humble arch was retained through a fantastically painstaking feat of engineering. And, yes, I damn well enjoyed a cigarette now as well.

While the Nervion river flowed unseen beyond that main stand opposite, those green hills were still visible away to my left. At both extremities of this East Stand were a couple of eccentric looking corner edifices, redolent of the Stadio Luigi Ferraris in Genoa and housing display screens. The roofs of both ends had joined with that of the main stand but their differing appearance, plus the fact that my stand was detached with those eccentricities abutting, denied any risk of the steeply two-tiered stadium's becoming any uniform bowl. And – unfortunately! – there was another very distinguishing feature. For all Wembley's lack of personality, its sightlines are flawless. Not so here in the Tribuna Este Alta where five pillars supported its roof and, from my seat level with the right eighteen-yard line, I'd forever have to peer around one of them to see developments in the centre-circle. Speaking of supporting structures, there were no floodlight pylons; as is the case with many Spanish stadia, the lighting was assembled within the roofs. When darkness descended later, this feature would also lend to some cathedral-like quality, although for now, before they filled up, I noticed too that most of the pews' red colour had become weather-worn and faded.

Time now to cast my mind.

o o o

Whereas the current crop had sauntered past the Guggenheim, almost half a century ago Valencia's players had strolled around Nottingham's city centre one afternoon and some of them, including Waldo their Brazilian star centre-forward, had popped into Boots on Pelham Street. My sister Patricia worked there in those days and at the tea table she told us all about it, how they'd gladly signed autographs for everyone who'd asked them. My ten-year-old mouth probably dropped its half-masticated food in excitement for I was a hunter as a child, whether outside The Hawthorns or Trent Bridge cricket ground. But, alas, I didn't get Waldo's signature or that of any other Valencia player, because Trisha hadn't asked them.

Seventeen years later Valencia would provide an altogether more uplifting experience, though. The hospitality afforded us the day before our match there was truly wonderful. We were shown all around inside the stadium including even the boardroom (I can remember seeing there a model of the Luis Casanova's proposed expansion, looking more like the towering Mestalla of today); we were presented with all kinds of club memorabilia; and to cap everything a chap with whom we'd got talking in a nearby bar had insisted upon driving us to his home where his missus cooked us a stew.

Back in October 1961 Valencia had slaughtered Forest on their way to winning two successive Inter-Cities Fairs' Cups, the forerunner of the UEFA Cup, which they'd lifted as well under Rafa Benitez in 2004, when they'd also won *La Liga* for the second time in three years. Their history – six Spanish championships and seven Spanish Cups, with a 1980 Cup-Winners' Cup triumph and two Champions League Final appearances at the start of the current decade thrown in for good measure too – was such that they held fourth ranking today among the most successful Spanish clubs of all time. But Ronald Koeman wasn't the happiest right now, for all that Valencia had won the *Copa del Rey* as recently as Wednesday night. For the club was currently in deep crisis.

At the start of the season hopes had been very high. '*Debemos luchar por el campeonato de Liga*' had been the clarion call of the long-serving attacking midfielder Miguel Angel Angulo: 'We must fight to be number one.' Since winning the league in 2004, Valencia had finished seventh, third and fourth. Come the early hours of Monday 29th October and the team was only four points off the top of the table. But it had just lost 0-3 in the Sanchez Pizjuan four days after being beaten 0-2 away by unfancied Rosenborg in the UEFA Champions League and, in those early hours, the coach Quique Sanchez Flores had been sacked by the then president Juan Bautista Soler. At a club notorious for the hot-seat nature of its coaches' office, for its fans' undoubted passion leaning towards impatient demand, and for internal strife not least where the dressing-room was concerned, Flores' dismissal was perhaps no big surprise, especially as how many fans had bemoaned his playing style as a dull one (in a city generally recognised as the partying capital of Spain); and especially given the domineering nature of the bulbous Soler. A fifty-one-year-old builder, he was currently in his fourth season at the helm and his tenure, in stark contrast to those years that immediately and richly had preceded it, had been barren, although he'd managed to more than double the club's already existing debt of £85 million whilst hiring and firing a handful of both coaches and sporting directors. It was now, all the more, heavy fist time. Soler had looked upon two men in particular, the captain David Albelda and the goalkeeper Santiago Canizares, both long-serving like Angulo, to be especially disruptive influences. The new coach he hired would quickly declare that all three had played their last games for the club: worrying all the more for Albelda who had his Euro 2008 holding midfielder's place to think of, and devastating too for Angulo who felt 'stabbed in the heart'. Koeman, that new coach, would prove to be not so much a new broom as some Dutch bull in a china shop – and disastrously so too. His first match in charge, in the Mestalla, was another humiliating 0-2 defeat by Rosenborg; Valencia would eventually finish bottom of their group and thus not even parachute into the UEFA Cup. As well as altering the personnel, Koeman attempted to have the team play in an alien 4-3-3 formation and, despite his banishment of those three perceived bad eggs, there would be voicings of discontent with that. The club now was one with a big I-am of a president (but a bumbling one at that), a big I-am of a coach (but a failing one at that), and a squad of players that was distinctly unhappy. The *Copa del Rey*, quite wondrously, would fly in the face of it all, Barcelona being put out narrowly in the semi-final before, despite Getafe clawing their way back into it, Valencia's 3-1 triumph in the final itself being underpinned by an opening twenty-five minutes of total domination, a whirlwind of intense determination that seemed to exorcise demons aside from earning a two-goal lead. By this time, on March 12th, Soler had resigned too.

Perhaps that trophy would form a rallying cry now. Valencia certainly needed one. Prior to this match in the San Mames, Koeman's record in charge where the league was concerned read: played twenty-one, won four, lost eleven. The coach who was hired not only to endow the team with a new unity, a new spirit, and not only to bring more silverware to the club's trophy room, but also to do that through an attractive style of play that would hearten the fans, had overseen a process which so far had endowed the Mestalla with just eleven home goals in as many games there. Eighteen points from twenty-one matches was relegation form. Under Koeman, Valencia had plummeted from fourth place to fifteenth today: two points above the trapdoor. The club hadn't been out of the top flight since 1931. Chaos really had become a crisis.

Tonight, doubtless like Koeman, I'd be looking for at least a buoyant determination where Valencia's players were concerned.

But I was more interested in Bilbao's, the current embodiment of a club's policy that flew in the face of much more than mere crisis. Where present-day football was concerned, it flew in the face of just about everything.

O O O

The club's idiosyncratic modus operandi is inextricably wound into the region's ethos, its sense of separateness; and indeed its politics. Towards the end of the nineteenth century, with those *fueros* denied them, and also with the region's becoming swamped now by folk from other parts of Spain to find work in the area's industrial revolution, a renewed nationalism was afoot: the Basque Nationalist Party (PNV) was formed in 1894. Four years later, heavily influenced by the strange but captivating sight of Englishmen indulging in this new pastime that was football, Athletic Club Bilbao came into being. (It's a moot point whether their eventual red and white striped shirts copied those of Sunderland, there being many north-easterners working in the local iron mines and foundries; or those of Southampton, there being many from that area working in the local shipyards; or whether such cloth, left over from making mattresses, was merely the cheapest option.)

For all that the club was born out of an English connection (and its Anglophilia survives to this day, though doubtless many ETA members with their links to Irish nationalists feel differently), it soon became an operation whereby the feeling of being a Basque could be given focus: since 1912, Athletic have indeed fielded only Basques. In 1936 a former Athletic player, Jose Antonio Aguirre, one of many with dual membership of the club and the PNV, was elected the first president of a legitimate Basque autonomous government within the framework of the central Republican government in Madrid, and since then all Athletic presidents have been PNV members. Following that horrific Civil War – during which the nearby town of Guernica, the ancient and spiritual heart of Basquedom, had been infamously flattened by Hitler's bombers – the brutal suppression by Franco's dictatorship served to provoke a yet keener sense of identity inside: one that, whilst *Euskara* had been banned and the club forced to adopt the Castilian name of Atletico, could be given vent inside the San Mames.

Identity wasn't the only heartwarmer that *La Catedral* provided, though. There was immense pride too in the actual footballing deeds. Whilst Valencia stand a laudable fourth in that all-time list, Athletic Club Bilbao can boast third. The honours list reads: eight times champions of Spain (twice during the Franco years); twenty-three times Spanish Cup winners (nine during the Franco years); five league and cup doubles (two during the Franco years); eighty-nine players (third most behind Real and Barca) provided for the Spanish national team. Since the birth of *La Liga* in 1929 only three clubs have never been relegated and Athletic are one of those. Noteworthy too is that they reached a European final in 1977, the UEFA Cup, when they lost out to Juventus only on away goals.

A major reason for that Anglophilia (and San Mames was originally laid with English turf) lies with Wolverhampton-born Fred Pentland, one of numerous Brits – others included Jimmy Hogan, Jesse Carver and George Raynor – who performed admirable coaching deeds abroad while such a craft remained viewed with disdain in the UK. A disciple of a short-passing style of play with which he indoctrinated Athletic, Pentland led the club to the double in both 1930 and 1931 as well as to a couple of runners-up spots and three more Cup victories. Nicknamed '*El Bombin*' on account of his trademark bowler hat, Pentland would be held in so much affection in Bilbao that not only was a testimonial game staged on his behalf in 1959 but also, upon his passing away three years later, a memorial service was held at San Mames in his honour.

Athletic's coaches over the years have included two more Englishmen in Ronnie Allen (one of Albion's greatest ever players) and Howard Kendall, plus a Slovak, a Serb and a German among others. In such capacity, the club has demonstrated its non-aversion to foreigners. But the policy which defines the club, that one which flies in the face of just about everything, is the refusal to allow anyone who isn't a Basque to play for it. Its disparagers might consider such a policy to be chauvinistic bordering on xenophobic. Its defenders, on the other hand, would consider its credo to be simply a pure one, and laud it all the more today as a bastion of virtue in a footballing landscape where distastefulness is all too prevalent. Even its defenders, though, might think that Athletic are doing themselves no favours any more. Going all-Basque in 1912 was one thing, but staying all-Basque into the twenty-first century was hardly a recipe for winning top prizes. Indeed, Athletic have won nothing since their last double year of 1984 and, of course, in the meantime, the likes of Real and Barca have bought virtually whomever they fancied at whatever financial cost, while the likes of Villarreal have gone shopping in South America. But is trophy-hunting their priority anyway? In his introduction to the club's centenary book, their then president Jose Maria Arrate spoke of Athletic's being 'more than a football club, it is a feeling' with ways that 'often escape rational analysis'. He continued: 'We only wish for the sons of our soil to represent our club, and in so wishing we stand out as a sporting entity, not a business concept.' Bearing out those last four words, the red and white stripes are still unbesmirched by any sponsor's name ten years later: purity indeed. (To a cynic's eye, even Barcelona would seem to be engaged in a priming exercise by planting Unicef upon their own shirts.)

In truth, Athletic's policy has become more flexible in recent years, the criteria for qualification widening: you could play for Athletic so long as you were just of Basque descent, or hailed from Basque provinces other than merely Vizcaya, or indeed even if you'd only landed in the region as a nipper but learnt your stuff there. Thus did the Brazilian-born Biurrun don the goalkeeper's shirt in the 1980s, while Bixente Lizarazu played sixteen matches in the 1996-7 season before leaving for Bayern Munich (allegedly under threat from ETA for not contributing to its cause). In 1995 meanwhile, Athletic's prising of Joseba Etxeberria from Real Sociedad's *cantera* (which translates literally as 'quarry' but can also denote a club's catchment area or, particularly, its youth scheme) led to ill-feeling in Guipuzcoa province, which now saw Athletic in a high-handed light. Real Sociedad, though, had already abandoned its own Basques-only policy six years earlier when signing John Aldridge, and other Basque clubs such as Osasuna and Alaves have between them fielded several foreigners over the years, Sammy Lee famously bemoaning that his first training session with the former team had involved diving practice, while the latter's line-up in the 2001 UEFA Cup Final had included the likes of Cosmin Contra and Jordi Cruyff.

Thus is Athletic – and virtually half of the entire population of the Basque Country lives in the Greater Bilbao metropolitan area – viewed as the chief proponent of, and synonymous with, Basqueness where football's concerned. In *Ghosts Of Spain*, Giles Tremlett wrote of the Basques: 'There is something deeply attractive, dashing even, about a small group of people proudly defending their culture in a globalising world.' For all the accusations, those words could apply also to Athletic Club Bilbao in today's football world.

○ ○ ○

As kick-off approached, exhortation blasted over the tannoy in *Euskara*, followed by the club anthem likewise with its words displayed on those screens for everyone to join in – which they did. Thirty-four thousand was the given attendance figure tonight, though San Mames' forty-thousand capacity hadn't looked quite that underpopulated to my eye. Despite their having thronged Madrid the other night, I detected no Valencia fans here at all. OK, there are huge distances to cover across Spain and this is doubtless a reason for not attending away matches; plus, with most *Primera* games' being played on Sunday nights, and given those distances involved, there's the matter of work in the morning. Yet I still find the paucity of visiting fans in Spain something of a conundrum. And right now Valencia could certainly have done with some encouragement; maybe just the sight of a pocket of hardy, determined souls might have helped as a spur in what was now a relegation battle.

Bilbao's players formed a guard of honour to welcome the new Cup holders onto the pitch and the crowd warmly joined in the applause. The home side was virtually at full strength although the declining Asier del Horno, now back at the club on loan from Valencia themselves, was absent. I'd noticed del Horno years earlier when watching Sky's coverage and, dreaming on, wondered if Albion, then new to the Premier League, might have considered making an offer for that young, tall, accomplished left-back. But then his reputation grew and Chelsea fancied him, so Chelsea had him, until they replaced him with the till-then underpaid Ashley Cole. For Valencia's part, eight players who'd started in Madrid also started here: Hildebrand and left-back Moretti had picked up knocks against Getafe while the forward Silva was suspended. Hildebrand's replacement was the thirty-four-year-old Juan Luis Mora who, in his previous match away to Zaragoza four months earlier, had given away a penalty and notched an own-goal; *Marca*, not mincing its words, had described the former as an absurd lack of judgement and the latter, in failing to deal with a harmless-looking cross, as a *'chiste'* – a joke. Valencia tonight wore orange shirts and socks with blue shorts, so at least those blue tops outside the Guggenheim had carried a bit of relevance, though I thought this strip smacked just a little of a pub team's.

In my mind's eye I'd tended to look upon Athletic over the years as a big, physical team not averse to meting out the odd hard knock, particularly so – and putting it mildly – where centre-back Andoni Goikoetxea was concerned. Goikoetxea had been a linchpin of the rather dour and abrasive team which Javier Clemente took to the Spanish title in 1983 and that double the following season. The coach now was Joaquin Caparros, who'd been Juande Ramos' predecessor at Sevilla but considered there by some to be rather too defensive-minded. When I'd watched Bilbao lose 1–3 at the Camp Nou back in September on television, they'd looked, as Harry Redknapp might euphemistically have put it, 'average'. In the past two seasons they'd had serious brushes with unthinkable relegation, and survival in 2007 had been ensured only on the very last day with a 2–0 defeat of Levante at San Mames. Tonight, albeit with fixtures running out, they were still only six points clear of the drop themselves, having lost 0–3 away to resurgent Deportivo the previous weekend amid a few question marks over their attitude. Whilst I was looking for buoyant determination on the part of Valencia's players, I was wondering too what these sons of the soil were really made of now.

O O O

In the eighteenth minute, having started much the brighter, Bilbao took the lead. They'd had a loud penalty shout for handball dismissed by Rubinos Perez, the referee I'd seen five weeks earlier down in Almeria, but immediately the ball had landed at the feet of Javi Martinez on the edge of the box, and his powerful shot was deflected past Mora by centre-back Raul Albiol. Martinez would have an excellent game in central midfield, forceful and intelligent, which indeed epitomised Bilbao tonight.

Koeman had abandoned his previously imposed formation (as indeed he had for the Cup Final), setting up Valencia now in a way favoured by so many Spanish coaches: 4-2-3-1, with David Villa up top. It didn't work. Bilbao looked sharp, confident and more determined, gobbling up most loose balls; Valencia seemed anything but buoyant and, despite some inevitable nice touches, looked disjointed, Villa lacking support.

Such was the way of the first half, even though Koeman

would subsequently tell the media that he'd thought his team had been '*bien*' during that period, and even though he'd made changes at half-time. I've got nothing against Ronald Koeman. He was actually one of my favourite players, even though as a back defender I wouldn't have put him in any team upon which my life depended. Yet I loved watching him spray those unerring forty-yard passes and put away those free-kicks, dinked or powered. I'd just known, in Barca's finest hour at Wembley against Sampdoria, that he was going to burst the net with his missile, behind which I was smack in line. I fear, however, he may turn out now to be a bit like Bryan Robson (the best all-round midfield player I've ever seen, and scorer of a famously quick goal at the San Mames for England against France in that 1982 World Cup): great on the pitch but 'average' off it. I hope I'm wrong.

There was no roar when Bilbao reappeared for the second half, just applause. Midfielder Fran Yeste had suffered an ankle injury and was now replaced by Joseba Garmendia. Koeman's two changes meanwhile had involved the introduction of Joaquin, the highly talented and much-capped right-winger but recently out of favour at the Mestalla, and Fernando Morientes, who'd been quite prolific at the Bernabeu but considered not sufficiently *galactico* prior to stuttering under Benitez at Anfield. Those making way included Hedwiges Maduro, a young Dutchman brought in by Koeman from Ajax to replace Albelda, but who'd been sadly anonymous here. With Mata – a youngster drafted in by Quique Sanchez Flores from Real Madrid's B-team during the summer, and rated highly enough by Valencia for a 60 million euros buy-out clause to be stamped upon him – pushed wider and higher, Koeman had now gone virtually 4-2-4. On the evidence of the first half, the wisdom of this escaped me; surely they'd have been better served by bolstering instead of denuding the midfield in the face of Bilbao's solid dominance, trying to keep more of the ball, trying to be more cohesive (and determined) in saving the game.

They got punished big-time. Just three minutes into the second period Bilbao scored a cracking goal that lifted me out of my seat, working the ball around, then very cute build-up play up the right flank in front of me involving the impressive Susaeta, then a neat turn on the corner of the box by the outstanding Etxeberria who slipped a low ball in to the near post, where the tall, blond and mobile centre-forward Llorente slid it home. Whilst Schuster on Real Madrid's bench tends to lean back, Koeman habitually hunches forward, and now he rubbed his head while, without throwing in their towel, Valencia's players' visibly dropped.

Koeman would say afterwards to the media, too, that in the second half it was as though his team were playing with '*cinco arriba y cinco atras*': five up front and five at the back. Chasing the game now, they became even more disjointed, with big holes in midfield into which Bilbao poured with relish. After sixty-five minutes it was 3-0. In the Vizcaya edition of *El Correo*, the journalist Juan Pablo Martin would say sympathetically that the first and third goals were examples of how luck can desert a struggling team, but I thought this third goal again demonstrated Valencia's lack of resolve. Llorente's attempted lob was kept out by poor Mora but in the resultant melee it was Bilbao who wanted it more and Llorente tucked the ball away.

Five minutes later Koeman made his last substitution, Mata replaced by Edu, and three minutes after that Valencia reduced the deficit with another deflected goal, this time David Villa's free-kick from the edge of the area flying past Armando via the head of young centre-back Fernando Amorebieta, who'd dealt firmly with anything that the opposition could muster.

The Bilbao fans (and this was yet another instance of females galore, three young ones on the row directly in front and a middle-aged one immediately to my right with husband and son, all of them bedecked) had struck me throughout as warm of nature, even polite, and certainly appreciative of the finer points of the game. Their team tonight was playing some attractive stuff, and showing real neatness and patience in wanting to retain possession for all the basic forcefulness. I'd wondered how they'd found Clemente's rather circumspect and rough team of old, but then that team had been winners; and tonight the locals left no doubt that they appreciated, too, determination and strength, a player busting a gut to win the ball back or coming out tops from a fifty-fifty challenge drawing special applause. With ten minutes remaining, there was a particularly intriguing moment inside the San Mames.

Away to my right behind that goal, towards the bottom, were Athletic's most vociferous supporters, with an *ikurrina* (the red, green and white Basque flag) or three to accompany them. These supporters suddenly came out with a piercing chant. Everyone else fell into a hush, save for the odd murmur. It was difficult to tell whether such reaction was born of deference here, or disapproving dismay there, or not wanting to reveal one's own leanings. A couple of men seated directly behind me, whom I'd recognised as conversing in *Euskara*, were among the silent. One middle-aged man a few rows in front, though remaining seated, eventually broke into a ripple of subdued applause, as if he at least had the courage of his convictions. I obviously couldn't understand the words of that chant, but I had no doubt it was in support of ETA (who'd been at it again today). Then the chanters moved seamlessly into one of '*Ath-le-tic*!! *Ath-le-tic*!!' which was readily and deafeningly taken up by all, maybe in not only homage but also some relief.

Within five minutes Bilbao notched a fourth goal, a rather embarrassing one. There was a big hole inside their penalty area now which none other than the right-back, Iraola, burst into. Albiol opted to launch into a sliding tackle, Iraola rode it, then rifled the ball inside Mora's near post.

In the last minute it became 5-1, and this goal was very embarrassing indeed. Etxeberria chased a long ball up the right, got there, eschewed taking it to the corner flag, evaded Portuguese left-back Caneira all too easily, and crossed on the turn. There were at least three orange shirts in the box but only one of Athletic: Aduriz, who'd replaced Llorente just prior to Valencia's goal. Aduriz it was who met the centre and flicked a header across Mora.

I was amazed by the volume of debris left behind: carrier bags, food remnants, wrapping paper, newspapers, plastic water bottles and, yes, beer cans. And, most probably, surely inevitably, Ronald Koeman's tenure.

The next morning's *Marca*, with a pun on Athletic's nickname, would headline its match report: '*Koeman esta para los leones*' (Koeman's for the lions). It quoted the man who'd stepped into Soler's shoes, Agustin Morera, as saying that no decisions would be taken in the heat of the moment. Only a couple of Valencia's players had been given more than one out of three in *Marca*'s ratings (five had received zero): Joaquin for his second-half strivings, and the Portuguese right-back Miguel, who'd indeed caught my eye as being both strong and accomplished, not least in his forays.

For Athletic's part, this was the first time that they'd scored five goals in a league game at San Mames since June 1999, and it put them nine points clear of the drop with five matches remaining: surely now no repeat of last season's near-disaster. Indeed, such had been the performance here that the president, Fernando Garcia Macua, would speak in *El Correo* of renewed hope for the future, an Athletic team more like its former self, one with that strong identity on the pitch for which it was renowned, one that had waned dangerously over the past couple of years.

○ ○ ○

The weather forecast eventually became true now, Sunday evening's light showers giving way to Monday's grey sky and steady rain, a day for idling away time until my early evening flight home by dodging from bar to bar, reading the newspapers, and taking in the scenes. There was no escaping Athletic. The coffee in my first port of call came with a sugar sachet that had red and white stripes and bore the legend: '*Cafe oficial del Athletic Club*'. It also carried a shadowy figure in ball-striking pose, who might well have been the legendary Pichichi. Meanwhile the league table showed Real Madrid ten points clear at the top – of Villarreal, with Barcelona a point behind them. Sevilla, despite that damaging home defeat, were now only three points off a Champions League slot – and Almeria were now only three points behind them. Three points also separated Osasuna in fourteenth from Recreativo in the dreaded eighteenth; a dogfight was in store, with Valencia, Valladolid and a crumpling Zaragoza – though they'd just beaten Recre 3-0 at home – in the thick of it too.

And: there was no escaping ETA.

Depending on your persuasion, they were either steadfast pursuers of Basque freedom or a nefarious blot on the landscape. The broad political landscape since the new post-Franco democratic constitution had come into being back in 1978 was that Spain, whilst that constitution was founded upon the oneness of the Spanish nation, consisted of seventeen regions each of which enjoyed a sizeable chunk of self-government: one of those regions being the Basque Country (controlled by the PNV), or rather those four Spanish provinces that were part of it. Not enough for ETA, who in any case consider their dream of total self-determination to include three French provinces too. Whilst the PNV in 2003 had demanded a referendum on the creation of a Basque state, ETA continues its terrorists' campaign. Since its formation in 1959 with the intention of being at the very least a thorn in Franco's side, it has been the cause of over 850 deaths, both innocents and those who are deemed to oppose them, the most recent that of a former socialist councillor in Guipuzcoa on the eve of last month's general election. One assassination was historic: in 1973 ETA killed Franco's earmarked successor of the same ilk, which ultimately saw Juan Carlos instead lead the country into democracy. In March 2004, meanwhile, prime minister Aznar had arguably lost that general election through having wrongly and expediently insisted that ETA was to blame for the horrendous Madrid train bombings; when the truth was revealed, that it was the work of Islamists, the outraged electorate blamed an evasive Aznar for having sided, against all public opinion, with Presidents Bush and Blair over Iraq.

Recent opinion polls showed that roughly one third of Basques wanted a separate state, a third wanted Spain to be a federation, and the other third were content with the status quo. One cannot help but believe, though, especially given that harrowing Civil War of not so very long ago with all that it's touched them, that the vast majority of folk in Spain, including Basques, simply abhor violence of any sort. ETA is on dodgy ground in more ways than one.

And so, on Sunday, although without any casualties, its three-kilo bomb had destroyed the local headquarters of the Basque Socialist Party (one obviously not to its liking) in the town of Elgoibar, also in Guipuzcoa.

○ ○ ○

At around 5pm on this Monday I stepped outside the airport building to light up and the only other person on the benches was an old man in his eighties wearing a black beret, and all he had with him were a carrier bag and an umbrella. At his age he would have seen it all. He just sat there gazing now at the verdant, rain-sodden hills before eventually shuffling away towards them. I hadn't known where he'd come from and I didn't know where he was going, but he looked proud and content. He'd seemed to say something, even though he hadn't spoken.

What of Athletic themselves? As someone who knows all too well himself the reality of today's football but despite all that remains true to his cause, I for one take my hat off to them; and if I had a thousand hats I'd take them all off. My time here, yes, had caused Athletic Club Bilbao to now become my favourite 'Spanish' team. Sorry, Sevilla. If I'd wanted a 'different corner', I'd found it here more than anywhere else.

If they remain true to their principles, they'll surely never be champions of Spain ever again – although, Spanish football being how it is, a UEFA Champions League place is entirely feasible. For, and even though last season had been the worst in the club's history, I'd like to believe that the Basque Country is such a fertile hotbed that players good enough will always come through. The evidence of this Valencia match reinforced such belief. I hope, for the sake of Macua and the fathers of those four-year-old girls I'd seen wearing the shirt by the river, that they will. But even if somehow they weren't to, the thought of Athletic's support waning, come what may, is an impossible one.

Some *pueblo*. Some support. Deeper than the Nervion river, higher than those hills.

9

NEW WORLDS
Sunday 18th May

On the evening of 3rd August 1492, Christopher Columbus had set sail with local crews from Palos de la Frontera to land in what would become known as the New World.

In December 1889, just a couple of miles along the coast, Spain's first tennis club was founded in the city of Huelva by British residents. Two years later, just north of that city, British residents also built Spain's first golf course.

Whilst Huelva can thus take some credit for the birth of the Americas as we now recognise them and also for the introduction of sports that would lead ultimately to the likes of Manuel Santana and Rafael Nadal or Seve Ballesteros and Sergio Garcia bestriding those particular worlds, the city is also highly significant for another reason. The multi-billion euro, stellar world that is today's Spanish football was born here too.

Being a history enthusiast I was always going to pay this place a visit. I'd certainly chosen my moment: a relegation scrap on the final day of the *Primera Division's* season.

○ ○ ○

Though not quite to the same degree as Columbus, who'd believed his bold voyage had instead discovered a sea route to the East Indies, I was stepping rather into the unknown myself now. As had been the case with my trip to Almeria a couple of months earlier, I hadn't been sure whether I'd be able even to get to Huelva never mind get a ticket for the match. I hadn't used the train because its infrequent timetable was unaccommodating and, when I'd attempted to book a coach seat online, the computer screen had instructed me to get off immediately because there was a problem with the coach company's web security certificate. As for buying a match ticket online: no chance. The coach journey was via Seville and, given such a popular destination, the time of day (Saturday afternoon), and indeed the sparsity of this service too, I stepped into Malaga's coach station somewhat unconfidently.

As it turned out the coach was less than half-full for three hours and forty-five minutes of soporific tedium, wholly in contrast to that Almeria route, but so anticipated because I remembered the view from my train window when I'd travelled to Seville back in September. The only eye-catching sight as the motorway carried me relentlessly through an albeit green but flat and largely lifeless landscape was a curious roadsign: one that told me it was now 85 kilometres to Huelva and 133 to Portugal. I couldn't recall ever seeing a sign that held the name of just a country itself as opposed to that of some frontier town, and certainly not where it mentioned an actual city in the same breath. The sign seemed to underline Huelva's isolation, that those eighty-five kilometres held nothing – which indeed they didn't – until you eventually reached its back-of-beyondness, as if it were somehow quarantined, and then all of forty-eight kilometres after that you'd come across another nation that enjoyed keeping its distance too. Well, I for one will stick up for Huelva. There are some roadsigns in England that delight in conveying a city's marketed appeal or indeed its self-importance, dubiously so in some cases. For instance, the proclamation that Coventry, other than for its horrific bombing, is 'historic' has never rung true with me. OK, the inventor of the jet engine was born there, but that story of some long-haired eleventh-century woman indulging in a spot of nude equestrianism was always a tall one and in any case it hardly constituted the Charge of the Light Brigade. But if ever a city might have advertised its genuine significance as you approached it then Huelva would surely have fitted the bill. Huelva, however, hadn't done so and, over the next couple of days, it would indeed strike me as being a wholly unpretentious place, even self-effacing, although I'd see proper pride in people's eyes when it came to football.

I finally got there at quarter-to-seven and, putting the finding of digs on a backburner, sought out a taxi rank. Deflation lay around the corner.

O O O

Three drivers were standing nattering atop a long row of a dozen cabs. The one who claimed me beckoned me to clamber inside and I told him that I wanted to go to the Estadio Nuevo Colombino, but before shoehorning myself into the front seat I asked him if he knew for sure whether its ticket office would be open at this hour. He shouted to his mates, one of whom stepped towards me and spoke some English. When I told him that, yes, I was after a ticket for tomorrow night's match against Valladolid, he said there were none left and emphasised the finality with a knowing and suitable gesture. It was as I'd rather expected. The club's somewhat limited website had fuelled my fears without my having been able to entirely decipher its information; this was a match where either team could end up dropping down to the second division; the Nuevo Colombino, to which the local fans were in any case bidding a fond farewell till next season, held only around twenty thousand. So: what to do now? Right now, I was going to fix myself up with somewhere to stay then step out to watch Frank Rijkaard's last game in charge of Barcelona. For tomorrow, my plan was this: get myself to the outskirts' stadium by ten in the morning, try the ticket office anyway, and look for any bars nearby. If there were indeed to be a bar close to the ground, I was going to return a good hour before kick-off to seek a tout; the bar, should it be screening the match, would be my fallback arrangement. No bars? No tout-seeking. Even though it'd feel a bit like cheating, I really wanted to see this match even if only on television. It wasn't one to be missed. But that was only one plan I had for tomorrow. On Sunday I was going on a history tour too.

There aren't many budget-friendly places to stay in Huelva; in fact I didn't see any at all. Eventually I staggered upon the Hotel Tartessos on the Avenida Martin Alonso Pinzon, whose four stars might suspiciously have been self-awarded, one of those places where a plentiful supply of headed stationery, a shower cap and an overpriced minibar (though no coffee) are considered to lift it above three or even two. I sneaked a look inside one of its conference rooms on my fourth floor and shuddered at the thought of spending a claustrophobic day on such a rudimentary chair. But the Tartessos was offering a weekend reduced rate and a hundred and thirty euros for two nights was OK by me. Come the morning, too, and I'd realise how conveniently I'd landed.

It was official by now that Hermo's lad and Barca were on the point of parting company. Tonight's game at already-relegated Murcia was a goal-fest, the visitors winning 5-3. The young Mexican forward Giovani dos Santos, who hadn't found the net all season, scored a hat-trick now and his second goal, a delicious chip under pressure from the edge of the box, drew a grin from Rijkaard so warm as to be fatherly. There were a couple of banners in the crowd thanking the coach for all he'd done, never mind that things had ultimately gone pear-shaped. Lluis' old hero, Guardiola, would be elevated from the B-team to take charge now, which seemed either a brave (given his inexperience) move or a foolish one (for the same reason) on the part of the persuasive president, Laporta, who himself was under heavy fire these days from the fans.

I ambled back to the hotel at around half-midnight and before taking the lift, on a whim, raised the matter of match tickets with the bloke on the desk. He said he felt sure he'd heard on the radio earlier that there were still a few left. I asked for a wake-up call for eight-thirty and rode upward with renewed hope.

O O O

Half a dozen or so visiting fans were hanging around outside the hotel entrance in their violet and white colours when I re-emerged. Some three hundred and fifty miles they'd come and I silently applauded them, even though they'd had no spare tickets.

Unsurprisingly there was hardly anyone around the stadium when I got there but a man pointed me in the direction of the ticket office, which wasn't readily locatable. At an outside corner was a wide flight of concrete steps, down which someone else was coming, and in confirming to me that the office was at the top he also warned me that tonight was a sell-out. I dragged myself up anyway and two other men were at the counter being dealt with. The old adage that you should never give up hope is one thing, but sometimes we plainly kid ourselves. There was a notice stuck on the window telling me clearly that all tickets for tonight's match had gone, information that was reiterated verbally now by a polite girl behind the counter. So why had something just been handed over to those men? She told me they'd just been collecting. So there's definitely no tickets left, right? Definitely no tickets left: they'd all gone by Wednesday. She smiled sympathetically. Any chance of sitting in the press box then? I had to repeat this last question. She shook her head and chuckled.

So that was that. Nor could I see any bars close by.

Would I have still set out yesterday had I known on Wednesday night? Before leaving the Nuevo Colombino I'd see things that made me feel more than glad I'd come here anyway; and back in the city centre there'd be another sight or two to behold.

○ ○ ○

A wide road skirted the Nuevo Colombino's main stand and across it, taking on an almost ethereal quality in the shimmering sunlight, were marshy waters formed by the confluence of the Odiel and Tinto river estuaries as they flowed towards the Gulf of Cadiz. Away to my left, towards the horizon and beyond, lay in turn the docks, Columbus' starting point and the huge wetland wilderness that was the Donana national park with all its ornithological delights. To my left also I could see belching white smoke, Franco's having foisted a petrochemical industry upon Huelva half a century earlier. But the sight that really captured me, after I'd trailed my eye across the waters and turned to my right, was the city's own heritage site, unused now except by promenaders, an old black wharf that jutted and curved into the estuary almost serenely for all its redundancy and rust, an indispensable monument to an era long-gone but which had been so famously instrumental towards the present.

That wharf had served as a shipping point for, especially, the copper that had been carried there by train from a mining area thirty-five miles or so north-east of Huelva. Today, the Rio Tinto Group's business empire involves operations on a global scale, including zinc and diamonds in Australia, aluminium in Canada and uranium in Namibia, but back in the early 1870s the opening venture of this new company had been in a region whose vast mineral wealth had long ago engaged Phoenicians and Romans but had subsequently been strangely ignored until its latterly being exploited less than efficiently by the wearied Spanish. Cue a British-dominated syndicate to seize a main chance, taking its company name from the Tinto river that flowed through the area.

The romantic notion is that of English gentlemen bestowing upon the locals a new prosperity, and introducing them too to those unknown sporting pursuits as a kind of philanthropic thank-you for their own serious enrichment. The reality, though, would seem to be rather different. Even in recent years the Rio Tinto Group's policies have led to a blemished image, particularly in the matter of human rights, and back in its Andalucian infancy it'd had no qualms in relocating an entire village, having dynamited the original that stood in its way. A snobbish (to say the very least) attitude, too, is evidenced by the construction of exclusive residential quarters that forcibly barred native mineworkers, and by the rigorous discouragement of any complicating liaison with native women. One such exclusive quarter was the Barrio de Bella Vista, whose Great War memorial would salute just management staff. It's almost enough to make you wonder that maybe rugger, instead of football, might have become deemed the preferred way of things here, unless of course all that manly grappling and forever hauling yourself back up from the floor was looked upon as a decided no-no under the searing Andalucian sun, rugger not exactly being a game where you can let the ball do the work. Nor, though, as Phil Ball points out in *Morbo*, was football exactly high on the agenda when the Huelva residents of the Rio Tinto Mining Company finally got round to forming an official recreation club in December 1889. Football would eventually have become established in Spain in any case – events in Bilbao would surely have seen to that – which is probably why Huelva doesn't seem to receive all the warm credit it deserves, especially given the modern club's less than prolific record and thus low profile. But, for all Rio Tinto's self-centredness, the fact that its employees introduced not only tennis and golf but also football to Spaniards – even if only by signal – is indisputable; and Huelva's present-day pride, untrumpeted though it might be, is well placed indeed, for not only did its menfolk sail with Columbus but they also responded to that signal before any others did.

I legged it back into the city centre feeling frustrated but warmed. Wherever I've been, I've never been one for taking many photographs. I see people swanning around special places interested only, it seems, in capturing those places on film, as if a record is more valuable than a living, memorable experience, but my preference is the latter. Now, though, I took a photo, one that (hopefully) would show the distant Nuevo Colombino through the framework of the elevated railroad as it made for the wharf: acorns and oaks and all that. A few yards up the road and I couldn't help but be impressed by Huelva's train station, a quite beautiful neo-Moorish building that dated from 1880, its construction funded by Rio Tinto and the place from where Huelva Recreation Club – including two Spaniards – had set out in March 1890 for Seville and the very first officially recorded football match in Spain. Back in the city centre and just a stone's throw from my hotel, I'd see where it really had all begun, however imprecisely – despite the self-effacing absence of anything so much as a plaque outside.

Casa Colon – Columbus House – is one of those edifices that manage to appear welcoming for all their formality, its decidedly authoritative style softened by its pastel brown facade with white facings, its air calmed by lilac and palm trees. Today it serves as a conference and cultural centre, and stands with all its drapes and bunting on the Avenida Martin Alonso Pinzon just before that main road becomes the Alameda Sundheim: two historic names indeed. Pinzon had been captain of one of Columbus' ships that set out from Palos, while the Anglo-German William Sundheim had played a crucial role in raising the finance to get Rio Tinto up and running. Sundheim it was who also arranged a meeting just before Christmas 1889 in the Casa Colon, at that time Rio Tinto's main headquarters, the meeting where Huelva

Recreation Club was launched to provide a structure enabling expats to gather sociably on dates that would feature events like tennis, athletics and, er, dining. Many a football had been kicked around already up by the mines (and by men laying the railway line), ever since Rio Tinto had first got hold of them, so even though management had forbade dallying with local damsels it'd at least been tolerant of a bit of soccer by the workers and, to be fair, there is evidence that indeed some of the white-collar individuals themselves enjoyed turning out too. But there is no evidence of football being raised at the Casa Colon's meeting (nor, indeed, rugger). So can this meeting really be looked upon as the founding of Real Club Recreativo de Huelva, the football club which is the oldest in Spain, and the birth of that country's beautiful game? Well, it's surely not an unsafe assumption that the night of 23rd December 1889 provided at least germination where football was concerned, whether at the nosh-up that immediately followed the meeting or very soon after that, because within a week space had been made next to the Casa Colon for a team drawn from the newly formed Club's members to play a football match against a visiting ship's crew. On that basis, I'd say the answer to that question is affirmative enough. The Seville trip a few weeks later indicates that these footballers wanted to keep it going, too: which they certainly did.

Before I'd left the Nuevo Colombino I'd stumbled across a treasure trove in its bowels. I'd found access to the pitch so that at least I could, well, take some photos: 1889 had been emblazoned across both ends, while the pitch's condition was just begging for action, making me wish I were at least twenty years younger. A stern voice soon ordered me to leave but as I did so, to the left of the main stand, there was a door ajar, and another voice that wasn't stern in the slightest allowed me inside. The old chap was busy doing some polishing but didn't mind my looking around the room, beyond which was a bar area. I'd found myself inside Recre's Veterans' Club, and this room was Recre's history.

Among the records mounted on the walls was one listing the founding years of Spain's earliest clubs, illustrating how an outfit such as Recre kept that signal at green until the heavyweights of today reacted, Spain's taking up of football a slow process until the turn of the twentieth century (nor was the Spanish FA founded until as late as 1913, while *La Liga's* inception wasn't till 1929). There was no mention of Aguilas, a little club from Murcia province currently struggling along at the third level and born back in 1896, nor, understandably, of any other perhaps innumerable minnows that had first kicked a football in those nascent days and waved a flag; the wall's list was confined to clubs that were easily recognisable. Recre 1889; then Bilbao 1898, Barcelona 1899, Espanyol 1900, Real Madrid 1902. It was pride without boasting, for the listing was just matter-of-factly presented amid all the other stuff on display.

Other charted information included the fact that the club's first stadium, El Velodromo, had been officially inaugurated back in 1892 – the fourth centenary of Columbus' first expedition – by Queen Maria Cristina and her son Alfonso XIII; seventeen years later Alfonso would become honorary president and bestow the *Real* prefix. By then, in 1903, Huelva Recreation Club had become *espanoliza* and renamed Club Recreativo de Huelva, the Britishness transmuting into Spanishness now, although Dr Alexander McKay would oversee the transition, holding the post of president for three years until 1906.

More than anything else, though, it was the photographs that intrigued me, especially the old ones, and the room was full of them. One that caught my eye was of none other than the current national coach, Luis Aragones, who today appears recedingly grey, bespectacled and rather irascible, but as a twenty-year-old here looked burly with thick black hair during his loan at Recre from Real Madrid for the 1958-9 season. Another photo showed a Scotsman named Charles Adams, complete with big white moustache: Adams was the club's president from its founding up until handing over to McKay. By far the most fascinating photographs, however, were those countless ones of team groups dating all the way back to the club's earliest years. Unfortunately captions bearing years and players' names were few, but here was one such assembly in particular where all the players looked distinctly British, aged anything between early twenties and early forties, resplendent in striped shirts, and posing quite possibly by the Casa Colon. A chap on the front row sat rakishly in a beret without looking at the camera. A chap standing on the right of the back row meanwhile – and not the goalie, either – smiled proudly: all forty-odd years, seventeen stones and two chins of him, his shirt straining to contain his stomach and his shorts wondering what it was like to be baggy.

But it had, after all, been a recreation club, and many are the fat forty-year-old couch potatoes today who've never kicked a ball.

○ ○ ○

A few more Valladolid supporters had been standing outside the train station and several were congregating in the city centre now, sitting outside bars that had taken their time in opening but by one o'clock were starting to get busy in the sunshine. By two o'clock the Recre fans had begun to show their colours too and the match, a 6pm kick-off, was filling the air. I was sat next to a lounging group of visitors as one Recre fan came along honking his car horn, scarf dangling, and he slowed down to shout something from his window. But it wasn't abuse, nor even aimed at Valladolid, it was an unkind remark about Osasuna who themselves were in grave danger tonight, and the Recre fan drove away guffawing and honking again while the visitors laughed and clapped him. Still no spare tickets though.

When I walked past the Casa Colon, there was a young woman pushing a pram whose occupant was shielded by a parasol in Recre's blue and white. Little could messrs Sundheim, Adams and McKay have known, I thought to myself, although they'd surely have been truly gobsmacked had they been inside the Bernabeu seventeen months ago when Recre slew Real Madrid there 3-0, reportedly in front of no less than three thousand travelling fans too, and this on a Wednesday night as well. That said, not even the current president, a builder named Francisco Mendoza, had taken himself to the Bernabeu that night, and indeed he'd wanted the game to be postponed: 'Football matters the least at this time,' he'd said. Tragically, a fans' coach had collided with a truck not long after setting out in the early morning, and four had been killed.

Recre's history, though, for all the special status involved, has rendered the club one for whom the phrase 'out of sight, out of mind' might have been coined, which could perhaps apply to the city itself given the remoteness of its location. Recreativo have won no trophies and the Spanish national team has never drawn upon them. As recently as 1998 they'd been in the *Segunda Division B*, the third level, backwaters to which they were well used. Until last season they'd only ever twice sampled a campaign in the top flight, 1979 and 2003 bringing instant demotion, although in the latter year they'd managed to reach their only *Copa del Rey* final, losing 0-3 to Mallorca. No player, aside perhaps from Aragones, has ever really made his mark at Recre prior to moving on and pulling up trees elsewhere, although Arsenal's Manuel Almunia had played a couple of games on loan here five seasons ago whilst another goalkeeper, the Hungarian Franz Platko, had long ago wound down his distinguished career in Huelva before eventually coaching the likes of Kubala and Suarez at Barca. That's largely it: Recre's forever plodding along and scratching around in obscurity, bless them. Nevertheless, things had improved recently. In 2001, the same year that the Nuevo Colombino was opened, Mendoza had taken over the presidency to oversee what is surely the best – however modest

– era since the club's founding. Whilst that demotion back in 1979 had led to a decade of stagnation in the second division prior to several worse years of toil in *Segunda B*, relegation in 2003 (not forgetting their cup final appearance either) seemed to fire a new determination not to sink back into oblivion. Two top-six finishes were followed by the second division championship in 2006, and last season Recre had quite astoundingly finished eighth. But for a poor end to the season, only five points from the last twenty-one available, and they might even have earned a UEFA Cup place too. Unfortunately, the young coach Marcelino Garcia had been tempted to Racing de Santander that summer; his successor Victor Munoz had struggled and already departed; and tonight Recre were fighting for their *Primera* lives.

As also were Real Valladolid, who'd achieved rather more since first kicking a ball as late as 1928, even reaching a Cup-Winners' Cup quarter-final in 1990. Although they too had never lifted a major trophy – both of their *Copa del Rey* finals had been losing ones – their thirty-eight seasons spent in the top flight had elevated them to as high as thirteenth in Spain's all-time rankings, and some notable players had worn their shirt over the years: Sanchis and Hierro of Real Madrid fame, goalkeeper Antonio Ramallets of Barca fame, the eccentric Colombians Carlos Valderrama and Rene Higuita, while Luis Garcia had played here in his pre-Liverpool days and Valladolid had also been Gabriel Heinze's first European club. Relegated four years ago, they'd stormed to the second division title last season, but this reacquaintance with the *Primera* had been spent checking to see how close was the third-bottom team.

Right now, with Murcia and financially-crippled Levante long gone, that third-bottom team was Zaragoza, who'd finished sixth last term and had probably held hopes of securing a Champions League place for next season; given the talent at their disposal, Roberto Ayala and Pablo Aimar to name but a couple, their slump was quite astonishing. They currently had forty-two points, one less than both Osasuna and Recreativo, while Valladolid had forty-four. (Valencia, post-Koeman, duly sacked after the debacle at the San Mames, had pulled clear.) Both Zaragoza and Osasuna had difficult away games tonight, the former at Mallorca who had the division's top goalscorer in Daniel Guiza, and the latter at Santander where Racing – trying to stave off Mallorca themselves – were playing for a first ever European place. Permutations were numerous but, as far as Recre were concerned, whilst even defeat might prove OK, only victory would leave no question.

What I needed to do now myself was to find a bar that was definitely going to show the game, which unsurprisingly was pay-per-view.

○ ○ ○

There was a brief downpour half an hour before kick-off, which I'd managed to dodge because I was already inside the bar, a smart one across the road from my hotel and quite peacefully named *Dehesa Santa Maria*, the word *dehesa* meaning 'pasture'. I was amid only a handful to begin with and thus seized prime position, a high stool at perfect distance from the TV and a ledge on my left to lean upon. Below the screen, draped over the cigarettes machine, was a blue and white scarf bearing the words '*Decano Del Futbol Espanyol*'. Often used in the same breath as Recre, *decano* translates literally as 'dean' but it also denotes 'senior member': respect duly paid.

The television cameras panned around the crowd, most of whom seemed to be eating monkey nuts in the revived sunshine, and the tannoy was belting out Gloria Gaynor's *I Will Survive*. At six o'clock two things particularly were on my mind: annoyingly, there were a few empty seats (maybe some season ticket holders had neither shown nor lent); and, bafflingly, there were no players to be seen.

That brief shower of rain had been nothing compared with what had been going on elsewhere; or so it transpired. Whilst the

TV informed us merely that the three matches in Huelva, Mallorca and Santander would all now kick off an hour late at 7pm – and then cheerfully suspended its coverage, leaving us to gawp at a blank screen while still wondering why – we subsequently learned that there'd been a deluge in Palma and they'd needed to clear the pitch.

I flicked through a couple of newspapers. *Huelva Informacion* said that the Recre Supporters' Federation had received a message of goodwill from Sevilla fans – '*deseo que el Decano continue entre los grandes del futbol espanol*' – and also that there'd be only a hundred and fifty Valladolid fans present tonight, which I'd found surprising given the numbers I'd already seen for myself. *Marca* – which on Saturday had dwelt big-time on the fact that its beloved Real Madrid was providing just two players, neither of whom was Raul, for Aragones' Euro 2008 squad – delivered the predictable quotes from the two coaches. Manolo Zambrano, who'd stepped in for Munoz, was saying that no attention would be paid to events further afield, that Recre would be focusing only on their own job in hand. Jose Luis Mendilibar, meanwhile, was stressing that Valladolid's objective tonight was a win, even though a draw would suffice. Since the television was currently pictureless, I also tried to envisage again the scene at the modestly smart stadium, an open two-tiered bowl except for the tall roofed main stand that bestrode the place and prevented uniformity. But then I thought of those empty seats again, wished I were there, and tried to think of the benefits of my situation. The only one I could really come up with was that I'd surely be kept abreast of those events further afield. Yes, I'll know all what's going on, I told myself, just before my left elbow missed that ledge.

O O O

Recre, crucially, had done themselves a massive favour the previous weekend by winning 2-0 at Almeria. But they'd been fortunate too, because I'd watched Zaragoza's 2-2 home draw with Real Madrid on television and Zaragoza, unfazed and determined, had deserved better, performing very well indeed and creating several scoring opportunities that went begging through a mixture of poor finishing, bad luck and Jerzy Dudek's playing out of his skin on a rare appearance in goal. Tonight, though, Recre looked a bag of nerves. Not so Valladolid, wearing black here. Mendilibar, who could count Helenio Herrera and Rafael Benitez among his predecessors, had evidently prepared his team well: they seemed composed from the off.

After fifteen minutes the cameras showed the Nuevo Colombino bouncing, and then the flashing caption: Mallorca 1 Zaragoza 0. Inevitably the scorer was Guiza, Jerez-born and who'd actually played four games on loan at Recre five seasons ago. Inside the bar, now quite crowded with folk of any age and either sex, including a couple of infants wearing the striped shirt, this development was greeted by polite applause, a bit like that you often hear from Spaniards when their aeroplane touches down in one piece. There was no other news from elsewhere during the rest of the first half, while the complexion of the game here remained the same, the visitors comfy and Recre looking like poor flyers. Five minutes before the break there was a development here too: Valladolid went ahead. Right-back Pedro Lopez centred, it looked to me as though Recre's centre-back Martin Caceres – a young Uruguayan on loan from Villarreal and coveted by Real Madrid – might have blocked it, but the ball reached Joseba Llorente and the centre-forward scored with a free diving header from close range, a good header though because the ball had been slightly behind him.

Ten minutes into the second half things got worse: the Brazilian international Ricardo Oliveira equalised for Zaragoza, and the caption now showed Recre in the bottom three. The groans became those of anguished disbelief just seconds later after Sinama-Pongolle, who'd previously had much trouble finding the net at either Anfield Road or Ewood Park, but had scored a cracker in Almeria, went round Valladolid's 'keeper Asenjo. '*Gol!!*' filled the jumping bar. But, seemingly impossibly, Sinama-Pongolle had blazed wide of the gaping net. Shortly afterwards he was through on Asenjo again, this time screwing his shot across the face of the goal. It was the Frenchman's last act. He'd picked up a slight knee strain in training the day before and now limped off.

Recre had made their first substitution only just beforehand, and both men involved perhaps offered a further illustration of how the club had hopefully left its backwater existence behind, its profile a bit more upswing now. The young man who went off was Marco Ruben, an Argentinian forward also on loan from Villarreal and for whom River Plate had previously forked out the equivalent of five million pounds, no less. His replacement was the Turkish international Ersen Martin, latterly quite prolific for Trabzonspor, and whose recent protracted transfer had seen FIFA become involved.

Ersen quickly made his presence felt now with a low snapshot that Asenjo somehow deflected clear, the ball spinning over his goalframe. Gnashing of teeth and fearful sighing inside the Dehesa soon gave way to glee (and more clapping), though. Nine minutes after pulling level, Zaragoza fell behind again, Webo the scorer. But the tension was still acute, the game still bitty, the quality still poor, Recre still full of anxiety. Ersen, however, would become very influential, his determined running and all-round piercing play infusing the others with new spirit and verve. With seven minutes left on the clock, Zambrano made his third change, bringing on a forward, Varela, for the right-back, Pablo Oliveira.

After eighty-six minutes there was a loud shout from somewhere behind me. Nothing such had beaten the TV to it before, so perhaps this chap's radio had been on the blink, but it was surely another goal elsewhere in Recre's favour. And then the caption: Racing 1 Osasuna 0. Recre now had two scorelines to help them out.

Ersen then ran clean through the middle, only for Asenjo to foil him again. Three minutes into stoppage time he was at it once more, this time wriggling his way up the left. His low ball into the goalmouth was met by Sinama-Pongolle's replacement, Javi Guerrero. 1-1 and uproar in the bar. Almost immediately another caption: Mallorca 3 Zaragoza 1. An old boy to my right blew in relief.

Oliveira, again, would pull one back in Palma, Zaragoza's last convulsion; but all the scoring – and the *Primera Division* season too – was now over. *El Decano* was looking at an unprecedented third consecutive season in the top flight.

If there was rapture in the Pasture here, then back at the Nuevo Colombino there was pandemonium, the pitch invaded by ecstatic fans, a few Valladolid supporters cheerfully getting in on the act too, and Recre's players being chaired – and stripped. Quite rightly the special hero was Ersen the galvaniser. I'd guessed he might have had a rather difficult time of it in years gone by as a Turk brought up in Germany; though he'd started out with FC Nurnberg, he'd left for Turkey at the age of twenty, which was nine years ago by now. I looked at him, feted here by these Spaniards, and felt happy for him. Very soon, everyone in the Dehesa would look at him and roar with laughter. When Ersen finally left the pitch, all he had on were his underpants and his – strangely pulled up – socks. He looked very sinewy. I'm afraid I couldn't help but think then of that proud fat bloke of more than a century earlier.

○ ○ ○

There was a coach back to Malaga at eight in the morning, and other than that one I didn't know. Sod the coach. I wasn't getting up that early – even if I were capable – and I wasn't leaving Huelva so soon, because there were historic places that I still wanted to see. There had to be a train. There was: at twenty-to-three. Ample time to explore further and avail myself of newspapers.

The thing that got me was the level of passion. Watching neutrally a game merely on television, you can't possibly experience it. Looking at those newspapers now, their photographs, and there it was in all its depth, explosion and numbers. I hadn't known that Recre meant so very much to so many. While the editorial in *Viva Huelva*, a freebie, launched into overdrive about '*la identidad de un pueblo albiazul*', how Recre binds together the townsfolk whoever they are with all of their lives' worries and crises – which, of course, a football club can indeed do – here were the images in evidence. Even before the kick-off hundreds had assembled outside the stadium to greet the team coach upon its arrival – Mayor Pedro Rodriguez, suitably bedecked, had been among them – and last night the fountain on the Avenida de Andalucia was the gathering point for an estimated five thousand to soak in celebration well into the hours of darkness: a scene visited by the team coach too as it made its way to a group dinner. A close-up in *Huelva Deportiva* of the coach's occupants proved that they weren't just paying lip service either. Zambrano and the rest genuinely looked as though they'd have loved to jump in themselves. It was almost as if Recre had just won a trophy.

Although *Odiel* paid due attention to more pragmatic matters – Zambrano had admitted it was the worst performance of the season, while there were the questions of whether Mendoza would give him the job full-time and how Recre would replenish their squad with so many loanees now leaving – it too displayed the unbridled joy at the fountain. After all the agony and relief of Sunday, after a season of fear that it might sink back, much-loved *El Decano* was still among the elite.

○ ○ ○

The Rough Guide To Spain (its April 2004 edition anyway) describes Huelva as 'the least attractive and least interesting of Andalucia's provincial capitals'. Least interesting? I suppose it all depends upon what you might or might not be interested in. For myself, I'd respond to that disparagement by borrowing the immortal words of Sir Alf Ramsey when someone at Glasgow airport had bid him 'welcome' to Scotland: 'You must be fucking joking.'

Least attractive? OK, it's hardly blessed with the grandeur of Seville, but then it isn't likely to be since it was virtually demolished by an earthquake in the mid-eighteenth century. But I came upon enough pretty little *plazas* to give the city a pleasant air and enough churches to aid tranquillity. And then there's its quirkiness. Imagine you're strolling around, say, Plymouth, then all of a sudden you come across an arched gateway, and the arch bears the words 'King Alfonso XIII Quarter', beyond which lies a neighbourhood of typically Spanish dwellings dating from a hundred years ago. At the top of the Alameda Sundheim, an equivalent sight springs upon you. Commissioned by Rio Tinto in 1916 to house its more well-to-do British employees in home-from-home style, the *Barrio Reina Victoria* – still inhabited today – is a quite startling incongruity.

There was one more place I wanted to see before leaving, three hundred yards or so back down the Sundheim. The Veterans' Club had recorded that, between 1957 and the launching of their neat, white-atop-blue-seats new home seven years ago, Recre had plied their unsung trade at the little Estadio Municipal Colombino, inaugurated with a match against Athletic Bilbao. But it was their home previous to that I was interested in now, the place where Huelva Recreation Club had first provided itself with a designated sports arena, where the footballing activity had metamorphosed into a Spanish operation, where Recreativo had forever plodded along and scratched around in that obscurity for those sixty-five years: El Velodromo.

From the Alameda Sundheim it would easily be missed were it not for the set back presence of an open-air bar that helpfully bears the sign of '*Pena El Velodromo*'. Adjacent was a small grassy area holding a timeworn statue of a naked man in ball-kicking mode. The man himself looked old and I suspected it might well have been either Adams or McKay; given the revealing nature of the pose, though, such a statue would surely only have been put up in homage after their passing. Beyond the bar, just around a corner, lay an entrance above which was a small plate bearing a crest dated 1889 plus the inscriptions 'Real Club Recreativo de Tenis de Huelva' and 'Decano del Tenis Espanol'. Back in 1892 El Velodromo had indeed catered for tennis as well as football and cycling. Then, three years after the Rio Tinto mines had been handed back to Spain, the city council did away with the olden football pitch in 1957 and redeveloped the site as a civic sports centre, building in return as its name suggests the Municipal Colombino and leasing that to Recre. Today, though, the old Velodromo, lying between the Palace of Justice and the railway line, is a designated tennis club whose half a dozen clay courts are overlooked by a pleasant terrace and whose photographs in its bar include one or two that show Rafael Nadal's presence here. From my seat on the terrace it was difficult now to imagine men in their blue and white striped shirts playing football here, first the pioneers, then those Spaniards aware of their heritage but knowing also that what the club had so historically set in motion had left them trailing far, far behind. That all visible traces of yesteryear should have left this place made for a rather sad feeling, but then I thought again of yesterday's joy. Time and again the word 'permanencia' – to stay put – had cropped up over the weekend. But what Recre and their loyal fans really craved now was to have a lasting status among the big boys, a feeling I knew well myself.

My homeward journey involved changing trains in Seville, so for its first leg I'd follow that trail blazed back in March 1890. I was thinking of the future, however, when I spoke to the middle-aged chap behind the counter as he issued my ticket. I wished Recre good fortune and I can still see the glint in his eye.

Epilogue

The pressing need to feel something different inside where football's concerned wasn't one that I welcomed. I hadn't wanted, nor expected, football in England ever to end up dumping feelings of futility and distastefulness upon me. After all those years of being so tremendously engaged by it, from magic-kissed childhood through to still hopeful middle-age, I found such an outcome mournful. Who opens his arms in warm embrace of sadness? But you need to do something about sadness, and about sour tastes too. And my love of football is too strong to have given up on it.

In November 2007 Matthew Syed penned a lengthy piece in *The Times* in robust support of the English Premier League, thus rubbishing its critics: dinosaurs like myself. Syed doubtless would have considered his article to be very well reasoned, drawing as it did in support of his arguments upon (oh dear) financial data and the likes of, er, an 'authoritative survey' by Trinity College, Dublin. The main thrust of the article was that all the money swishing around the Premier League, especially from television revenues, is good for everyone in it: 'By compromising the ability of the top English clubs to compete successfully in the Champions League, it would erode the credibility of the Premier League around the world and enable Serie A and La Liga to poach disillusioned viewers', which in turn would have a detrimental effect upon the income of lesser clubs. Syed said too – using language in response to the accusers – that 'I rather like the football provided by today's globally capitalised, profit-obsessed, foreign-owned clubs'.

Syed didn't reveal which his favourite club was, or even if he had one, and nor did he say whether he actually took himself to matches as a spectator. The whole tone of his piece reminded me of an advert used to herald Sky TV's Ford Super Sunday: wide-eyed kids being driven in some sleek Ford car amid fluttering confetti to some squeaky-clean and posh celebrity event, Ford Super Sunday's being of course for the benefit of couch potatoes.

The reality of attending Premier League matches – and I attended every Albion match, home and away, for those three seasons that we've been part of it so far – is, in my opinion, rather different. In the 2002-3 season Albion fans were voted the Premier League's best (probably because we were viewed, a tad patronisingly, as being wholly determined to enjoy our inevitably brief stay), but a prevalent ditty of ours at that level was 'It's just like being in church'. Other than at Villa Park or St Andrew's on derby day, the only crowd that came anywhere near to reproducing the atmospheric rawness and vocal din of yesteryear was Everton's. At Highbury a fart would have been very audible. Roy Keane has famously described match day at Old Trafford. When I revisited Anfield the comparison with all those years ago was barely believable. As for Stamford Bridge, well, I won't ever be paying forty-eight quid to get cramp there again and see people sneeringly waving twenty-pound notes at me. When Albion played Manchester United at The Hawthorns, our sponsors tried to turn it into T-Mobile versus Vodafone. And all the time, of course – as at any ground in any division in England – there are the orange anoraks laying down the law, waiting to pounce.

Syed never touched upon the impossibility felt by a father on a less than affluent wage whose two young sons badger him to be taken to a Premier League match. But his most glaring, crucial, omission, one that marked him suspiciously as someone who sees football merely as entertainment and not as someone who loves his club to death, was the murder of any sport's lifeblood:

ambition. When I worked for The Football Association it really did try to be a governing body that oversaw English football for the greater good of everyone. Years later, in June 1991, The FA published *The Blueprint For The Future Of Football*, part of which proposed the formation of a new Premier League that would eventually comprise eighteen clubs, whose streamlined modus operandi would be beneficial to an apex-viewed national team, that league to be run by The FA itself (and which would also bring about finally the castration of a power-chasing Football League). In the climate of that time, The FA had feared a breakaway whose 'purpose would be to concentrate more commercial power in fewer clubs'. As David Lacey said in *The Guardian*: 'At least *The Blueprint* got that bit right.' Today the Premier League still comprises twenty clubs, its plethora of foreign players (338 at the last count, an average of 16.9 per squad) ever diminishes the number qualified to play for the national team, the Premier League runs English football, The FA hides behind its settee (when not dallying with its female clerks), and the Premier League has murdered ambition except for three or four of its twenty members, unless your ambition is to finish fourth. Yep, the Premier League is a great competition, Matthew. It must be, because it has all that money swishing around it. (And just a few weeks after Syed's piece came the revelation that it was chasing still more money: a proposal to play a thirty-ninth league game, the contestants probably to be seeded, those ten televised matches to be staged in five major cities around the globe. Who cares about the coherence of the competition? Who cares if a fan loath to miss a match can't afford to jet out to Hong Kong or Sydney? It would all be worth around another five million quid for each club while promulgating the 'brand'. Yep, the Premier League is a byword for integrity.)

My beloved Albion have just got promoted again to my despised Premier League. Yes of course I'm glad that we have done, but for one reason only. My life has spanned almost half that of English professional football itself and so, bias aside, I feel fairly qualified to say that West Bromwich Albion, historically and traditionally, belongs in the top tier of English football. When it's not there, it feels wrong. That is why I'm glad we're up there again. But I know we'll be wasting our time, just striving to stay there, the top four in a different world: futility. It's futile because realistic opportunity to win the top prizes and achieve real glory – like being champions of England – isn't there any more. I haven't dreamed for ages. The FA Cup? I'm afraid it's but a pale shadow of its former self. The top clubs treat it almost as some encumbrance and field their reserves; Blair and The FA even persuaded Manchester United not to enter it at all in 2000 because not to slight Blatter (whose nod to stage the 2006 World Cup was being chased) and his world club championship in Brazil that January was considered more important; the erstwhile grand occasion of the final has been wholly spoilt by playing the semis at Wembley too. As John Motson said in 2002: 'There's no point in pretending otherwise....other competitions, notably the Champions League in its inflated form....have buried the FA Cup.' Also the need to stay on the Premier League's gravy train, he might have added. I suspect the FA Cup has now become a bit like the League Cup in that not too many folk can even remember who won it a couple of years ago.

When I was on the coach from the West Midlands in April for our semi-final against Portsmouth, just about all I saw were balloons and face-painted kids on their way to Wem-ber-lee. Ditto a year earlier when we played Derby County in the play-offs final there. They might just as well have been on day trips to Alton Towers. I might be a dinosaur, but I used to love the minibus trips to away matches when we'd all get half-cut along a rumbustious way, maybe then have to dodge or deal with those who were unwelcoming, walk into some boozer and what the hell, enter some spirited and recognisable stadium, shout our proverbials off along with mostly everyone else to whom those ninety minutes meant all, while knowing that our dreams – our ambitions – weren't beyond us.

For the majority of my football-loving life so far, I'd been able to chase ambition on a level playing field in an atmosphere of rawness. All of that became denied to me.

I needed to find a different corner.

○ ○ ○

It's all relative. Right now Doncaster Rovers' fans (and indeed Hull City's) will be in rapture, but Leeds United's fans will have wanted to go on a bender for the wrong (or should that be right?) reasons. Take Care On The Steps, Leeds.

So what did I want from Spanish football? I only ever wanted to see if it could re-engage, The Baggies apart, my real love of the game. Aside from at the San Mames, I've been fortunate in that I've witnessed good contests. But of course I needed to feel inside much more than just that. In short, I was hoping for a matchday experience which would be as far removed as possible from the torpor of England's. And I also wanted to see, in my exploring, just how large was any futility factor.

So you reckon Spanish football is just Real and Barca with any others just scratching around beneath them? Villarreal have just finished second, ten points above Barcelona. Bear in mind two things, also. One: for three seasons after 2002-3, Real Madrid won nothing. Two: next season, Barca will be in the charge of a novice coach and reportedly without Ronaldinho, Deco and Eto'o, replacements required. Yes it's true that vacuums left by either club have historically more often than not been filled by the other, but it seems to me that vacuums in Spanish football allow filling by some chasing pack much more so than does English football. Could Everton ever finish second, ten points clear of third place? Next season, aside from Villarreal, the likes of Atletico, Sevilla and a sorted-out Valencia (under Unai

Emery) will be looking to push. That constitutes at least six teams with genuine ambition. And, perverse as this may sound, an opposite lends itself to the scenario too. Next season, Spain's second division will include Real Sociedad, Celta de Vigo and Real Zaragoza, all clubs with Champions League aspirations recently, the former two having been participants. There's a lot of flux in Spanish football. The more flux the better. Stagnation is one place from death.

Matchday experience? Christ.

Yes, the Bernabeu was rather inert, its air one of expectation and lacking edge. But elsewhere, especially at Sevilla and Almeria, I was amid raucousness and vitality, and such willing engagement would involve anyone and everyone around the stadium, unconfined to merely some main mob of choristers behind some goal. I saw no-one denied giving full vent to their feelings but nor did I see anyone get out of order, saw not one intervention by any puffed-up steward, saw not the slightest hint of any physical confrontation either inside or away from the stadium. It was a real delight to feel enveloped by such earthiness, earnestness and emotion. It all rekindled a sensation left so long behind in England that, upon first recognising it here, I'd realised that I'd clean forgotten what it was like: exhaustion. Even coming out of The Hawthorns hadn't held such property for ages, because that ground too has largely lost its verve. In the past I'd often come away from there knackered and so to then plonk myself down in some boozer would feel like some well-earned relief. But over these past few months, invariably having been among the very last to depart, stepping through the nut shells, the deserted stadium I was leaving seemed a place that was now all worn out, everything given, drained.

And then, above all, there's La Rosaleda. I applaud Athletic Bilbao's fans for their unshakeable loyalty. At the Sanchez Pizjuan the passion had been such that I'd been taken out of myself. But Malaga's supporters are something else.

I took myself to La Rosaleda once more on Sunday 15th June: the last day of the second division season. For much of the campaign Malaga had been marching relentlessly towards the *Primera's* door but for some time now had been spluttering, a prime example being four weeks earlier when, while I'd been in Huelva, they'd contrived to chuck away a 3-1 home lead against Hercules and lose astonishingly 4-6. Twenty-one thousand had been there that day and I'd have been interested to see their reaction. Two weeks later, in front of almost twenty thousand, they'd been held to a goalless draw by relegation-threatened Cadiz, whilst their penultimate game had produced the same scoreline at an also imperilled Granada 74, that club whose president had acquired Ciudad de Murcia in the previous close-season, had subsumed it into his own, and had basically bought its place in a higher division (yes, heinous things go on in Spain, too). But while Malaga had been fretting along the coast in Motril, favours were being done them elsewhere: Sporting de Gijon lost at Castellon, and Real Sociedad suicidally conceded two goals in stoppage time away to Alaves, turning three points into a 2-3 defeat. Thus, at kick-off on the final day, with Numancia already up, Sporting and Malaga each had sixty-nine points and Real Sociedad had sixty-seven.

I must say that I found the air of confidence outside the stadium surprising. The place was awash with blue and white but folk appeared to be bathing already in party mode. I checked my maths to see if I were somehow missing something, but here it was: if Real Sociedad beat Cordoba, if Sporting just drew with Eibar, and if Malaga choked enough to lose here to tenth-placed Tenerife, then.... Then again, Tenerife had won only once away all season. But then again that had been in Gijon, no less.

If many were feeling confident, no-one was being nonchalant. Thirty thousand had thronged to this one. And, genuinely, they were awesome.

Five thousand of them must have had horns. Horns were ablaze as I took my seat (yes, I'd gone to La Rosaleda four days earlier to make sure of a ticket), and they'd stay ablaze all through till after the last whistle. Never did they shut up. By the time Malaga's players came out for their final warm-up, the ground had virtually filled, the *Hinchas* were into their pogo dancing (and at almost six o'clock it was still hot), others around the arena were likewise at it, chanting was at full throttle. The leading Malaga player gesticulated, the decibel count rose even higher, there was a mass overhead swirling of scarves. A massive banner became unfurled behind the goal away to my left: '*Esta Noche Cenaremos En La Gloria*' (Tonight We Shall Dine On Glory). Immediately to my right was a fat-thighed man in his early forties, his young son, his wife and his pretty teenaged daughter. Between the four of them there was barely a moment's silence throughout (and the man had a horn, too). Throughout, from anywhere, incessantly, there was a racket, often fuelled further by a drum. Towards the end, at least two-thirds were doing the pogo. I thought to myself it was almost like being in South America. It was possibly the best support I'd ever witnessed any football team being given. It was certainly upbeat. It actually overstepped the mark because with stoppage time approaching several fans came onto the pitch and even dislodged the goalframe to my left in premature celebration. Now I saw just how many police were present as the referee took the players off. But there was absolutely no heavy-handedness, the invaders melted back, the goalframe was re-erected, the players eventually reappeared: and Tenerife scored. But Antonio Hidalgo had already scored twice, and Malaga were up.

I spared a thought for poor Real Sociedad, who five years earlier had let the championship of Spain itself slip through their fingers, two points short of Real Madrid in the end (and twenty ahead of Barcelona). Thirty-two-and-a-half thousand had gone to the Anoeta this evening but they'd only drawn – crucial for Cordoba who stayed up by the skin of their teeth. Had Cadiz not missed a stoppage-time penalty at Hercules, they'd have survived instead. How cruel is that?

O O O

No, I shan't be going to La Rosaleda too often next season, nor joining its *Guiri* (Foreigner) *Army*. I shall go there a couple of times, which will be like having a fix, but I'll be flying back to support Albion. What I really want to do is to continue exploring Spain and its football, because I've only just made a start. Which means that the novelty element will still be present.

Yes, I've asked myself searching questions where the element of novelty is concerned. Just how much has my enjoyment of the Spanish football scene been due to that? Unavoidably it's come into the equation, but it certainly hasn't been fundamental. My matchday experiences – despite that scarcity of away fans who would provide added pungency – have been genuinely pleasurable per se. The futility factor, meanwhile, is beyond such tentacles in any case. Villarreal would have bettered Barcelona by ten points whether I were living on the Costa del Sol or in Bartley Green.

For I have indeed enjoyed Spanish football so far and it has indeed, thankfully, enabled me to feel something different inside.

Of course it has its downsides, though. Funnily enough, the thing that right at the outset I'd feared might blight everything – so-called 'simulation', whether diving or feigning injury – hasn't been an issue so far. Again, I may have been fortunate in my choice of matches, but I recall those early antics of Iniesta and Melo at Almeria simply because no other instances come readily into mind. (Had Jose Mari turned out for Villarreal at the Bernabeu, I suspect more might.)

The Granada 74 case leaves a sour taste because, surely, such manoeuvring is ethically wrong on at least two counts: the purchasing of a higher station instead of earning it on the pitch, and the flagrant disregarding of fans' feelings. Both UEFA and FIFA were dismayed too and had tried to block the deal, but Carlos Marsa had been backed by the Court of Arbitration for

Sport. The worrying thing is that Spanish regulations permit such shenanigans. Maybe some measure of justice was done when Granada 74 duly dropped. (Antonio Tapia, having already left that club, then retook charge of Malaga, whence Muniz went to Santander to replace Marcelino, who'd departed for Zaragoza saying that he'd taken Racing as far as he could: which, in their particular case, is quite possibly true. Unai Emery had doubtless thought similarly in leaving Almeria. Whilst I stand by my opinion that Spain is more accommodating of challenge than is England, some can mount a more realistic challenge than others. But then again, it's only eight years ago that Villarreal were scraping their way out of the second division and within six years they'd go within a whisker of the Champions League final....)

Commercial imbalance? Yes, obviously. As we have seen in chapter five, and unlike in England, clubs in Spain are at liberty to negotiate their own individual TV deals, thus arming the bigger clubs with much more financial clout than others. Real Madrid, too, receive the equivalent of no less than twelve million pounds per year from their shirt sponsor bwin, the online betting company, which is almost double the amount that bwin pays AC Milan, quite a bit more than Getafe receive from Grupo Galco or Recreativo from Cepsa, and of course twelve million pounds more than Athletic Bilbao receive. If that belief of mine – that doors aren't padlocked in Spain – is a correct one, then all of this makes such a belief all the more a comforting thought. It's comforting to know that the likes of Betis and Osasuna have both qualified for the Champions League in the past three years.

That said, it does seem a rather onerous task to clamber out of Spain's lower divisions to reach the second; with good reason, the third level – *Segunda Division B* – is known as 'The Well'. Its four groups – loosely regionalised – comprise in total eighty clubs and promotion is decided via play-offs involving sixteen of them: winning a group guarantees nothing. As for the *Tercera Division*'s eighteen groups, they comprise no less than three hundred and sixty-four clubs. Real Oviedo had won their group by finishing sixteen points clear of second place. They went into the 72-club play-offs. In the first round's first leg they lost 1-4 away to a team named Caravaca who'd finished only fourth in their own group. A crowd of no less than 23,915 – this is Real Oviedo, whose fans love their club to death – flocked to the second leg. Oviedo won, but only 4-2, and they stayed put. And yet: even if you're ranked somewhere between 123rd and 486th in Spain – that is, down in the *Tercera* – it's thus possible to find yourself in the second division if you can achieve just two promotions. I haven't a clue which the 486th-ranked club is in England, but they won't be playing Wolves in two years' time.

In two years' time and for at least two more years after that, Spain will still be reigning European champions. They've just triumphed – and overcome their longstanding psychological barrier, basically one of fatalism – with a brand of play pleasing to the purist (though not surprising to those who watch domestic Spanish football): sturdy when not in possession and smart with the ball, loath to give it away but always striving to put it to cleverly hurtful use, two-footed players with awareness, intelligence and the reliable technique to underpin all that. To my mind, the real measure of a nation's footballing strength is not if a polyglot club side wins the UEFA Champions League but if the actual national team wins a championship. I don't see England winning titles until they at least eradicate, in the words of one of Capello's assistants, Franco Baldini, 'this culture after two or three passes of sailing the ball through the air like a crow'. Just how unified or otherwise are the Spanish peoples, meanwhile, is of course a highly debatable issue, but the patriotism on display around me during Euro 2008, particularly on the nights that Spain beat Russia to reach the final and then Germany to lift the trophy, was florid: open-topped cars jamming Fuengirola in their hundreds, especially along the Paseo Maritimo, flags aflight, horns ablaze, folk awhirl, foot-revellers echoing, bars awash.

There's a restaurant in Fuengirola's Picasso Square which I often use for my evening meal. Invariably there'll be half a dozen or so Spanish kids aged between eleven and thirteen playing around there with a ball. They don't just belt it against walls or scrap for it, they practise their tricks. Sometimes they form a circle and do a group keepy-uppy between them using feet, thighs, chests and heads. They love that ball and want to be smart with it, proficient. There are no adults telling them not to be so bloody fancy. I stuff another forkful into my mouth and make another kind of connection.

Scenes like those, and sights such as that chap running unprevented the entire length of La Rosaleda's Preferencia Stand with his massive flag, or such as a middle-aged woman named Pepa left entirely alone at Cadiz with her megaphone even to berate the visitors' bench, are heartwarming stuff. There's even something rather comforting in the knowledge that, in the season just ended, and for all Spain's own plentifulness of foreign players (184 in the top division at the last count, an average of 9.2 per squad), every single club president in the *Primera Division* was a Spaniard. No dubious Russians or Thais or on-the-make Americans. The majority of the coaches were Spanish, too. I'd come to feel a remoteness in England that I don't sense here. Thanks, Spain, for engaging me.

ABOUT THE AUTHOR

A football fan since the late 1950s, Richard Brentnall worked for The FA, has been a regular fanzine contributor, and played himself until, aged 38, a serious injury made him even slower. He now lives in southern Spain. This is his fourth book about the game.